By EDWARD F. DOLAN, Jr.

Basic
Football
Strategy

*An Introduction
for Young Players*

Foreword by Duffy Daugherty

*Illustrated with diagrams
by John Lane*

DOUBLEDAY & COMPANY, INC.   GARDEN CITY, NEW YORK

This book is for
John and Dorothy Wood

Library of Congress Cataloging in Publication Data

Dolan, Edward F   1924–
  Basic football strategy.

  (Basic strategy books)
  SUMMARY: An introduction to both offensive and
defensive football strategy as well as the mental
and physical preparation necessary to be a successful player.
    1. Football—Juvenile literature. [1. Foot-
ball]   I. Lane, John, 1932–   II. Title.
GV950.7.D64   796.33'22
ISBN 0-385-03998-0
        0-385-04184-5 Prebound
Library of Congress Catalog Card Number 76–3438

Contents

Foreword

There is one person in this world who can really make me angry. He's the fellow who tells me that young men need no more than hard muscles, wide shoulders, and strong legs to play football. In his opinion, brains just don't count out there on the field.

Nothing could be farther from the truth. It is certainly true that you must be in top physical shape if you hope to be a successful player, for football is a rough, body-contact sport. But after a lifetime spent in the game, I can tell you that you'll need far more than just brawn. You'll need to have a very good head on your shoulders.

Why?

Well, first and foremost, football is a game of strategy. Throughout all sixty minutes of play, you must never relax in your efforts to trick your opponent. On offense, you must constantly look for the moment when you can pull the surprise play—the pass when your opponent expects the run, and the run when he's thinking pass. On defense, you must always try to guess what the quarterback has in mind so that you can put a stop to his play immediately.

In a nutshell, unless you're intelligent and able to keep your head in the heat of play, you simply will not be up to applying all the offensive and defensive strategies necessary for a winning score.

Further, who will deny that football has become a complicated game over the years? There was a time when all teams lined up in pretty much the same way and used just a few plays. But now there are numerous offensive sets, numerous defensive alignments, and numerous plays and defenses. You need to know them all if you are to play your position expertly and confidently. Can you get the job done unless you're willing to put your head to the task of some hard study?

Next, football is a game of fundamentals, a game in which things must be done in the correct manner if they are to work effectively. There is a correct way to run with the football. A correct way to pass. A correct way to receive, intercept, or bat away a pass. A correct way to block. A correct way to tackle. All these fundamentals must be learned, perfected, and then remembered at all times. All this requires intelligence, not to mention a lion's share of self-discipline.

Finally, football is a game of winning attitudes. Every player must develop a sense of teamwork, a determination to win, a willingness to make the sacrifices necessary to keep in top physical condition, and an enthusiasm that will get his team back on the winning track when things go wrong. Winning attitudes are born in the head, not the muscles.

A knowledge of the game, a knowledge of football strategy, a mastery of the fundamentals, and the development of winning attitudes—all these mental factors must join with your physical strength and your natural athletic ability if you are to become a good player.

They are the keys to success on the field, and you'll find them all, plus much more, here in *Basic Football Strategy*. I know that they will be of great help in making you not only a hard-playing but also a fast-thinking football man.

And one more all-important point:

Whether you be a player or a spectator, this book will increase your enjoyment of football by giving you a greater understanding of the game. It's always more fun to participate in or watch a game when you know what's going on. And fun—that's what football is all about.

Offensive Strategy

1

SETTING UP
THE PLAY

Offensive formations: Every football play breaks from a formation. Today's offensive unit employs many formations, but not one of them is a haphazard arrangement of the men. Each is planned to set up the play in the most effective way possible.

Your coach will determine the various formations to be used by your team. Some will be best used for the pass. Some will best pave the way for the run. Some will enable you to pass or run with equal ease. All should pressure and, if possible, confuse the defense as to your plans.

You and the formations: One of your first jobs as a player is to learn your team's every formation and to know exactly where you fit into each. Only then will you be able to take your place quickly and confidently and thus keep the pressure on the defense. A moment's hesitation on your part will often be enough to spoil your unit's timing and give the defense a welcome edge.

To help you get started, this chapter will look at the formations most used in today's football. All can be varied in a number of ways to take advantage of certain game situations. We'll point out some of the variations as we go along.

The open set: You'll often hear this formation called the "pro set," for it is used by all professional teams. Employing a seven-man line, it sets a split end to one side, a tight end to the other, and a flankerback out beyond and to the rear of the tight end. The quarterback positions himself directly behind the center. The running backs usually stand about four yards farther back. Each is set on an invisible line that runs forward between his guard and tackle.

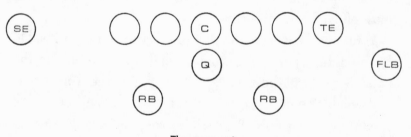

The open set

Though the split end is seen at the left above, and the flankerback at the right, you can reverse the two positions if you wish. Perhaps your flankerback is your top receiver and you find that coverage on the left is weak. You'd then send him out in that direction. Always set your team to hit at the defense's weakest spots.

The open set gives you two great advantages. First, with the flankerback and split end ready to jump off as wide receivers, it constantly threatens the pass. But, second, it also makes the defense think about the run, for the running backs are well positioned to hit off-tackle or straight ahead.

It does have a disadvantage, however, thanks to the fact that there are only two runners in the backfield. Should you try a quick hit to the inside, you'll find it difficult to have one back charge forward fast enough to lead the interference.

The spread set: A variation of the open set, this is a fine formation for passing plays. The flankerback and split end position themselves as before, but now the running backs move up just behind the line, one setting himself just beyond his tackle, the other just beyond the tight end. The quarterback now has five possible receivers up front. Heavy pass pressure is exerted on the defense.

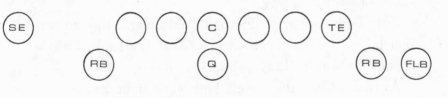

The spread set

You may vary the spread set so that only one running back moves up to the line. Even with just one back moved forward, you'd best still plan to pass. A run gives the defenders an advantage. They know that there are only two possible carriers—the quarterback, and the running back who has remained behind.

The twin set: Another variation of the open set, this formation pressures one side of the defense. The flanker-back moves from his original spot to a point near the split end. On the play, the flankerback and split end break away together and move into their pass routes. They use each other to free one man for the catch.

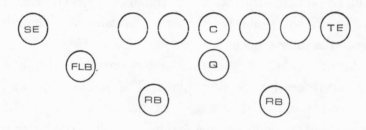

The twin set

The formation also threatens a run. The running backs, positioned as they are in the open set, can hit straight ahead or off-tackle.

The T-formation: A football "old-timer," this formation takes its name from the fact that the backs form a squat *T* behind the line.

As seen above, the *T* sets both ends tight and is best used for the run. One end or the other may be split, however, to increase the possibility of the pass.

But the run is still your best bet. In fact, a variety of running plays can break from the *T*. The halfbacks and fullback are positioned to hit the line at any point. Any

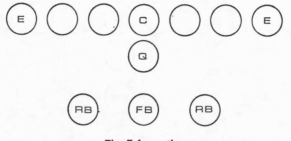

The *T*-formation

one of the backs is always on tap to lead the play. Fakes to one or two backs are constant threats.

The wishbone-T: Some coaches see the wishbone as a variation of the basic *T;* others call it a variation of the open set. Whatever the case may be, the formation sets a split end out to one side and moves the fullback forward until he is about three yards behind the quarterback. The wishbone is a fine formation for the hard-to-defend-against triple option. We'll run the play in the next chapter.

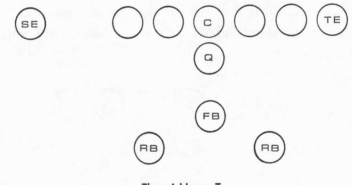

The wishbone-*T*

The I-formation: Here, the backs form yet another letter of the alphabet—this time the *I*. At times, you'll see all four backs in the *I*, giving the quarterback three possible carriers.

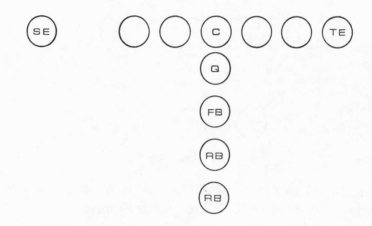

The *I*-formation—four backs

More often, however, you'll likely see the *I* take a shape that resembles the open set. The flankerback and split end move out to either side, while the running backs join the quarterback in the *I*. The first of the running backs drops into a three-point stance about three yards behind the quarterback and becomes a full-back. The second running back becomes a tailback. He takes a semi-upright stance so that he can see over the fullback. He stands about five yards behind the quarterback.

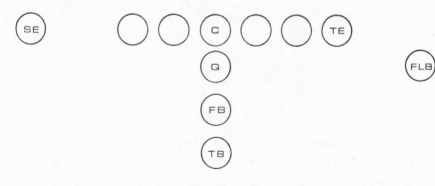

The *I*-formation—three backs

The formation is used for both the pass and the run. As does the open set, it sends the flankerback and split end out as wide receivers. For runs, the fullback can easily lead the tailback. Finally, the fullback himself can quickly hit inside.

Now, how can the *I* be varied?

The I-slot: With two exceptions, the *I*-slot is identical to the basic *I*. The exceptions: The tight end drops back about a yard and a half and becomes a wingback. The flankerback moves up to the line, becoming a split end.

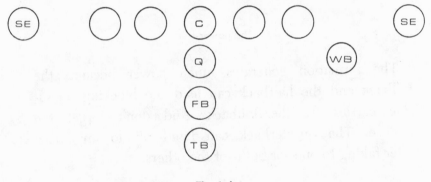

The *I*-slot

You can trigger a pass or a run from the formation. Various runs are possible, for all backs are available as carriers. A good bet also is the reverse. The wingback can quickly take the ball after the quarterback has faked the handoff to the fullback or the tailback.

The power-I: As its name suggests, this formation generates much forward power. You'll use it mainly on short yardage plays, especially when you're close to the defense's goal line.

For the power-*I*, the flankerback becomes a halfback,

moving to a spot about three and a half yards behind his tackle. You may split an end (as seen below) or play both tight.

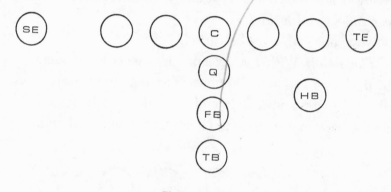

The power-*I*

The formation generates much power because the fullback and the halfback can lead the blocking on inside carries by the tailback. And don't forget the reverse. The quarterback can hand off to any back after faking to one—or both—of the others.

Learning the formations: Though the formations are many—and though they all can be varied—do not let them confuse you as you learn them. Each is nothing more than a way of arranging eleven men in a pattern prior to the play. To help yourself learn, look closely at the diagrams in this book and in your team's playbook. You'll soon see how each formation logically places each man to give the play its greatest strength. Once you see that logic, the formation should be easy to remember.

And don't be confused by the fact that some positions change their names from one formation to another, with the coach calling a player a flankerback on one and a fullback on another. There is nothing mysterious about the changing names. They simply indicate where a man is to play and the duties he is to perform.

So put your mind to learning all the formations and the position names and duties. With a little effort, you'll have them all down pat.

Tips

1. Learn all your team's formations.
2. Know exactly where you belong in each formation and be able to take your place in it quickly and confidently.
3. Do not let the number of your team's formations confuse you as you learn them. And do not be confused by the fact that some positions change their names from one formation to another.

2

THE RUNNING GAME

The ground attack: Your team must establish a successful ground attack as early in the game as possible. Your ability to move the ball on the ground will discourage the defense and give you confidence and momentum. Further, you'll soon be able to vary your plays between runs and passes, putting still more pressure on the defenders. They'll always have to be alert for the run and so will make the pass all the easier.

Should the defenders keep you from launching a solid ground attack, the advantage will be with them. Now you'll feel discouragement and they'll be the ones with the momentum. And they'll know that, sooner or later, you'll have to go to the air for needed yardage.

They'll be looking for the pass and will be in fine shape to intercept it or bat it away.

The plays used in your ground attack will be as many as your coaching staff can devise. With few exceptions, though, all will be founded on the basic running plays that you'll now meet in this chapter.

The line buck: This is the basic name given any play that sends the carrier ramming into the interior of the line between the two tackles. It most often nets short yardage, but can be turned into longer gains by a fleet runner who, with good blocks at the line, can break quickly into the secondary and then put on a powerful burst of speed.

The line buck is much favored when you're right on your opponent's goal line. The runner charges straight ahead between his guard and center, often throwing himself over the line and into the end zone.

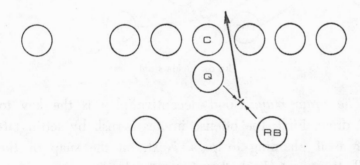

The line buck

The off-tackle slant: On this run, you travel somewhat wider than on the buck. You take the handoff from the quarterback and head on a diagonal to the outside of your right or left tackle. As is true of any play, the blocking here is all-important if you're to have any daylight for running. Your tight end and tackle hit their men and take them to the inside, clearing a path for you. Your fellow running back attends to the linebacker, while the flankerback heads downfield on a pass route and draws the cornerback off the play.

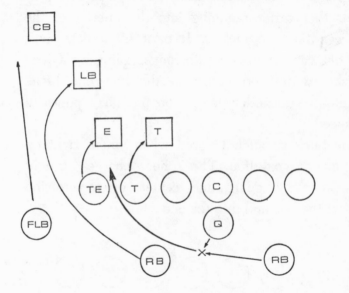

The off-tackle slant

The draw play: Good deceptive play is the key to the draw. First, the offense invites a rush by setting itself as if planning to pass. Next, on the snap of the ball, the quarterback drops straight back, pretending to move into the pocket. Third, the linemen put up a little resistance, but permit the defenders to charge into the backfield. The quarterback then hands off to you, and you slam past the defenders before they have the chance to halt their charge and grab you.

On the draw, always do everything you can to look as though a pass is planned. Invite a good rush. The success of the play depends on having the defenders charge fast and hard.

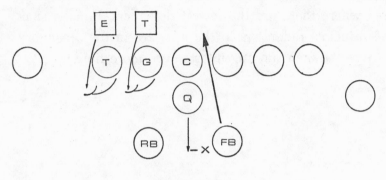

The draw play

The trap play: This run is similar to the draw and involves an element of deception. An offensive lineman deliberately allows his defender to break through the front wall. He drops back in front of the defender, then suddenly "traps" him by blocking him to the side. You run through the area left open by the block.

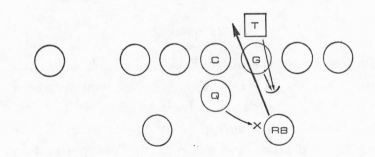

The trap play

The sweep: The sweep, which was once better known as the *end run*, has three advantages. First, it permits the carrier to build up much speed so that as he rounds the flank of the line—"turns the corner"—he is going full tilt into the secondary. Second, it aims the run at an area where there are the fewest defenders. Finally, since the principal defenders in the area are in the secondary, it gives the men running interference more time to get to them.

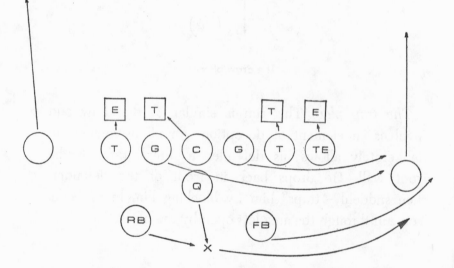

The sweep

On the sweep, the quarterback drops back and hands off or tosses the ball to you, after which you sprint for the flank. The guards come back off the line and join the fullback in setting up your interference. If the blockers on the line and those in the sweep can take care of their men or hold them back long enough, the play can result in a substantial gain.

The end-around reverse: Deception is added when
the sweep seems to start, but then turns into an end-
around reverse. Let's play you at split end over on the
right and see how the reverse works.

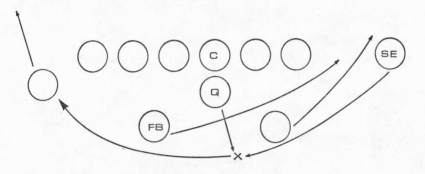

The end-around reverse

On taking the ball, the quarterback fakes a handoff
to the fullback, who then charges in your direction as
if running the sweep. The defense moves with him.
You then break from your spot and arc left across the
backfield. You meet the quarterback, take the handoff
from him, and head to the left of the line. It should be
well free of defenders.

Along with the carrier, the key man on the play is
the fullback. He must take the fake handoff convinc-
ingly and then run exactly as if he had the ball, drawing the defenders into pursuit. If he fails to attract
tacklers, he will not clear the left side of the line for
you. And if he does not fool them into thinking that he
has the ball, the defenders will immediately forget him
and key in on you.

The end-around is but one reverse in the offense's
bag of tricks. You may also use double and triple

reverses, with the direction of the play changing twice on the former, and three times on the latter. Let's take an example of a double reverse in which the quarterback runs to the right and hands off to a wingback moving to the left. The wingback then gives the ball to a running back traveling right.

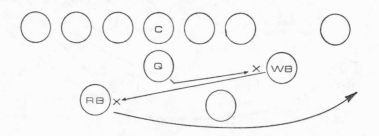

The double reverse

The quarterback option: This is one of the most effective plays in modern football. As its name indicates, it permits the quarterback to do either of two things with the ball: keep it himself or pitch it over to his running back. His choice depends entirely on what the defensive end does when the plays breaks.

Let's see the option in action.

As quarterback, you take the ball and head for the defensive end, with your running back moving along even with you but about five yards deep. Keep your eye on the defensive end the whole time. Remember, his actions will determine what you next do with the ball.

Suppose that he breaks through the line and charges you. Immediately toss the ball to your running back; he'll then head around the flank, free of the defensive end. But suppose that the defender suspects the toss

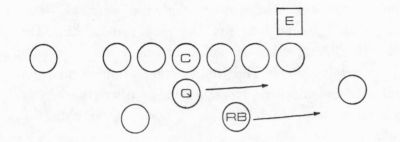

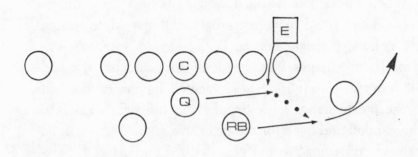

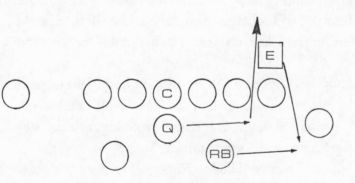

The quarterback option

and moves deep to the running back. Now you keep
the ball, turn upfield, and run through the area that he
has vacated.

The play has an advantage that never fails to charm

the quarterback. No matter what the defensive end does, you'll be able to run the play against him. He has two choices; either one will be wrong.

The triple option: The triple option promises to frustrate the defense even more. Again, as quarterback, you have a variety of choices as to what to do with the ball.

Here is the play worked from the wishbone-*T* and run to the right side of the line.

When the ball is snapped, you drop back on a diagonal to hand it off to your fullback. All the while, watch the defensive tackle, for he is the key to your first option. If he charges you, hand off to your fullback and let him run through the area vacated by the tackle. But if the tackle hangs back to take the fullback, then fake the handoff and head for the defensive end.

Now you complete the play with the quarterback option. Your running back will be following you. Should the defensive end charge him, keep the ball. Should the defensive end key on you, pitch out to the running back.

Thinking on offense: With these basic plays—and with the variations that can be made of them—you should be able to launch a strong running attack. But no matter how well your attack seems to be going, never become overconfident. Never ease the pressure. And never stop thinking. Remember all the plays you've tried in the game and figure out why they succeeded or failed. Do you need to change the angle of attack to turn a slant or a line buck from a failure to a success? If so, make the necessary adjustments. Did a

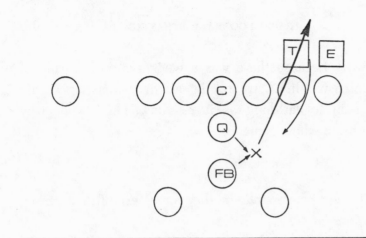

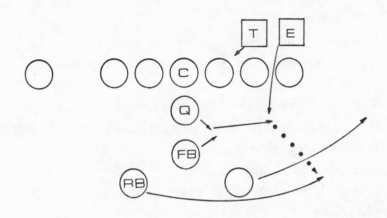

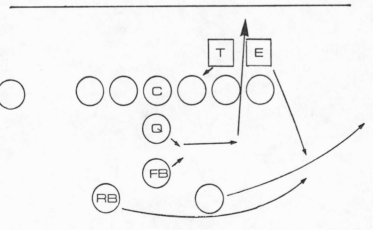

The triple option

play work because there was a weakness on one side of the defensive line? If so, hit at that weakness again and again for as long as it remains. Think your way through the whole game.

Tips

1. As soon as possible in the game, establish a strong ground attack.
2. On the draw, do everything to pretend that you plan a pass; draw the defense in and then scoot past their rush.
3. Remember the advantages of the sweep; it can result in a good gain if you manage to "turn the corner."
4. Keep your eye on the key defenders during any option play. See how they commit themselves. Then make the play accordingly.
5. Use your head at all times. Work successful runs again. Figure how to turn the failures into successes.

3

RUNNING WITH
THE BALL

Ball carriers: In the running plays of earlier years, the halfback provided speed, and the fullback power. The halfback, lightweight and agile, carried the ball on all plays demanding swiftness and deceptiveness—plays such as sweeps, reverses, and off-tackle slants. The fullback, heavy and broad-shouldered, took over when the line had to be charged head-on.

Today, however, the halfback and fullback are often classed together as "running backs," with each man expected to have *both* speed and power. If you're a halfback, your coach will want you to have not only the speed to turn the corner, but also the power to run the line. As a fullback, you'll continue to bull your way through the pit, but you'll also be handed a number of sweeps and reverses.

Speed and power are the running back's chief weapons. But the coach will also want you to be deceptive on your feet and determined to grind out every last yard on each carry. With runners possessing all these attributes, he can always be sure of mounting a solid and varied ground attack.

Further, the coach will demand that you know the fundamentals of running. These fundamentals set the rules for how best to carry the ball, rules that must be mastered by any running back who hopes to do anything but watch the game from the sidelines. So important are these rules that they will take up the rest of this chapter.

The stance: Before the ball is ever snapped, the first of the fundamentals is put to use. You take your stance in the formation, making sure that you take it correctly. It involves much more than just standing there and waiting for the play to break.

Your coach will employ one of two basic stances: the semi-upright or the three-point.

If he prefers the semi, you stand crouched over, with your knees slightly bent and your feet about eighteen inches apart and directly opposite each other. Your weight rides forward onto the balls of your feet. Your arms are straight and your hands rest just lightly on your knees.

Remember, *just lightly*. Do not put any weight on your hands, for then you'll tend to pitch forward. You'll have to pull up slightly when you start to move. A pre-

Semi-upright stance

cious second of forward motion will be lost—all that
the defense may need to stop the play.

When taking the three-point, you drop into a deep
crouch. One hand rests on the turf. Your feet are still
about eighteen inches apart, but now one is a comfortable distance behind the other, ready to plunge you
forward or to either side. If you're right-handed, your
right hand is on the ground and your right foot to the

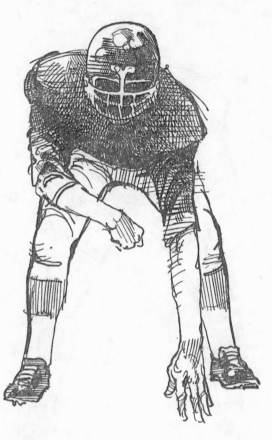

Three-point stance

rear. Your left forearm lies across your left leg, just above the knee. The hand and foot placements are reversed for southpaws.

Again, you must watch where you put your weight. Let it ride mainly on the inside half of the balls of your feet. Do not allow it to settle on your right hand, and do not drop down on your knuckles. You'll lose that precious second when you have to pull up as you begin to move. Rather, set your fingertips lightly against the ground and use them for balance only. In both the semi and the three-point, keep your head up so that you can see what the defense is doing.

Once you're in your stance, do nothing to give the play away. Do not unconsciously glance or face in the direction of the run. You may shift your weight to the side for a faster takeoff, but do not make the shift an obvious one. Avoid rubbing your hands together or flexing your fingers in anticipation of taking the ball. The defenders are constantly searching for clues as to what's coming, and they'll send you a thank-you letter for any wrong move.

In all, take your stance calmly. Set yourself so that you're comfortable. Square your body to the line. Keep your face a blank and your eyes straight ahead (unless your coach wants you to focus your gaze on the ball at the start of every play). Be ready to uncoil like a spring when the play breaks, but give nothing—absolutely nothing—away.

Taking the ball: On most running plays, the ball is snapped first to the quarterback, who then sends it on to you. In the instant that the play breaks, you move as fast as you can to the point of exchange. There, you receive the ball in one of two ways: The quarterback either hands it off or tosses it to you.

On the handoff, he places the ball gently against your stomach as you charge past with folded arms. You receive the toss on a lateral pitch as you head into your running route.

Let's look first at the fundamentals involved in taking the handoff.

The handoff: Correct body position

From the moment the play opens, you need to keep four points uppermost in mind.

First, make sure that your arms are positioned correctly to receive the ball. Suppose that you're to take the handoff from your right. Head for the quarterback with your right forearm across your chest and your left forearm across your waist. Cup your hands so that they will fit over the ends of the ball. As soon as you feel the handoff being made, fold your arms and hands about the ball and lock it securely against your body.

The position of your arms will be reversed when the handoff is made from your left.

Second, pay particular attention to the elbow on the handoff side. Hold it *up* and *out* from your body so that the ball will pass safely beneath and come to rest against your stomach. Should you drop the elbow as you approach the quarterback, the ball will likely strike it. The result will be a broken play or, worse, a fumble. The elbow drops automatically when you fold your arms about the ball.

Third, though you must move to the quarterback with all possible speed, don't try to reach him in one or two long strides. Instead, pumping your knees as you go, run with short, driving steps. They will give you plenty of speed and maximum control of your body. As you'll see in a moment, you'll need every ounce of body control as you head into the line.

Finally, never look at the ball as you take it. Always keep your eyes on what is taking shape in front of you. Otherwise, you'll be unable to take evasive action should a hole close or a tackler bear down on you. So learn to do what all good running backs do: Take the handoff by "feel" alone. Know when to expect the ball; know its slight thump as it comes against you; and know when to fold your arms about it. You will develop that "feel" by constantly practicing handoffs with your quarterback.

Now for the toss:

Again, move to the point of exchange as fast as possible. You'll start with short, driving steps, but at times —especially on the quarterback option—you may be pretty much at a full stride when the toss is made. Contrary to the handoff, you must now keep your eye on the ball. You must, as coaches say, "look the ball into your hands" as it comes your way, no matter who is closing on you. Take your eyes away for an instant and you're certain to miss or bobble the catch.

Hitting the line: Once you've taken the handoff, charge ahead along your route. Continue with those short, driving steps and look for the hole that is supposed to be opening in the line. If it's there, plunge through it—*fast.*

But let's say that it closes as you approach. Now you'll see the importance of those short, driving steps.

You've got to change direction *instantly,* sliding to the left or right. Those short steps will give you the body control necessary to do so. Were you at full stride, you'd never be able to shift in time, never be able to slip away from disaster and convert it into a solid gain or perhaps a score.

When you've taken the ball, keep it folded protectively in your arms for your first steps. As soon as you think it wise, however, shift the ball to one arm or the other. Be sure to tuck it in the arm that is away from the tacklers—your right arm if you're running to the right, your left if you're running to the left. It will then be safe from efforts to slap or hook it out of your grasp. Use your free arm to ward off tacklers.

In the secondary: Once you're through to the secondary, you need to think of three things: acceleration, your blockers, and running room. To accelerate, switch to a stride, driving yourself faster and faster until you're at top speed. Be prepared at all times to change direction, to fend off tacklers with a straight-arm, to fake them into wrong moves, and to twist away from them.

Do not, however, try to outrun your interference. Pick up your blockers, stay close behind them, and let them clear a path for you. Whenever you can do so, fake out a tackler in a way that puts him in a blocker's path. Once your blockers have done their work, then really put on a head of steam.

All the while, look for running room—"daylight." Always head for the spot where you see the fewest tacklers.

Finally, when some defender does get his hands on you, produce that all-important "second effort"—the determination to fight for every last inch before going down. Do all that you can not to let one man pull you to the ground. Even if you've got half a dozen tacklers on your back, carry them as far as possible, always fighting to break loose. Often, second effort marks the difference between victory and defeat.

Faking the handoff: One of the great arts of the runner is "faking the handoff." It is said to be an art because sharp-eyed defenders are anything but easy to fool. To outwit them, you must run as hard as if you actually have the ball. If you run "softly" to protect yourself against being hit hard, you'll betray the fake immediately. The defense will let you go and turn on the quarterback or the actual carrier.

On the fake, you're to head for the handoff point fast and curl around in front of the quarterback to hide his keeping action from the defense. At the right moment, grasp your elbows with your hands. This will give the defense the impression that you've got the ball. Then run hard—and keep running until you're tackled or until you hear the referee's whistle.

Tips

1. Learn and perfect the fundamentals of good running.
2. Take your stance correctly and do nothing to give the coming play away.
3. Get to the point of exchange as fast as possible.
4. Keep your eyes on the defenders when taking the handoff; keep your eyes on the ball when taking the toss.
5. Move to the point of exchange and then into the line with short, driving steps so that you will always have full body control and be able to change direction in an instant.
6. In the secondary, accelerate, take full advantage of your blockers, run for daylight, and come up with a mighty "second effort" when being tackled.

4

THE PASSING GAME

Pass routes: If executed correctly, the pass is a devastating offensive weapon. But it will work only if every man carries out his assignment. The blockers must protect the passer, giving him time to release the ball. The quarterback must throw on target in the fewest seconds possible. The receivers must run their routes and be in perfect position for the reception.

All-important are the routes. Receivers do not simply dash downfield as they please. Each follows a specific path that takes him to a specific area. Thanks to the routes, the quarterback always knows where each receiver should be and so is able to release the ball quickly and accurately.

As a receiver, you'll be called upon to run many

different routes. Let's look now at the basic ones, beginning with those used for the short gain.

The sideline pattern: Suppose that you're the receiver
and that six yards are needed for a first down. At the
snap of the ball, you sprint downfield for about eight
yards, causing the defender covering you in the secondary to turn so that you won't get behind him.

As he turns, put on the brakes. Plant your inside
foot, and angle back fast for the sideline. You should
receive the ball about seven yards distant from the line
of scrimmage and step out of bounds with a yard to
spare for the first down.

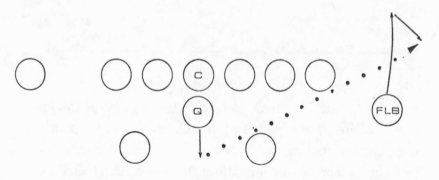

The sideline pattern

Constant practice will be needed to perfect the sideline pattern. You must always run more than the distance required for the first down and arrive at the sideline with at least a yard more than is needed—five
yards out from scrimmage if four are needed, nine if
eight are needed, and so on. The quarterback must
throw as you plant your inside foot. If he waits until
you are heading for the sideline, you'll likely be out of
bounds by the time the ball reaches you.

The hook: Let's say that, again, you need six yards for the first down. Take off downfield for eight yards, running just as you would on the sideline pattern. Charge as fast as you can just to the outside of the man covering you. As he moves to you, change your direction, "hooking" inside and taking a step or two back toward the line of scrimmage to receive the ball.

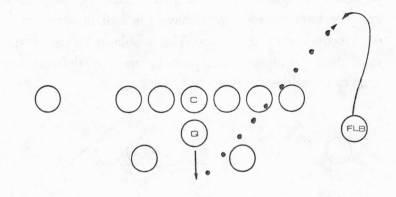

The inside hook

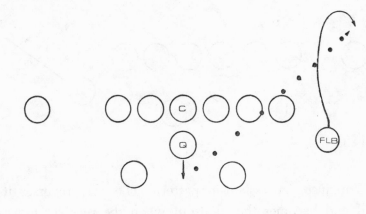

The outside hook

You may also hook to the outside. Whatever the
yardage needed for the first down, make sure that you
always hook and catch the ball with at least a yard to
spare. The hook is also known as the *buttonhook*, the
fishhook, and the *curl*.

The slant: This pattern is responsible for one of the
quickest passes in football. At the break of the play,
sprint at a forty-five-degree angle to the inside. Look
for the ball right away. The quarterback will step back
and fire immediately. You'll have the ball in your hands
one second after the snap. The whole purpose of the
slant is to complete the pass before the defense has
time to cover the receiver.

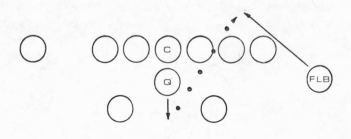

Slant-in

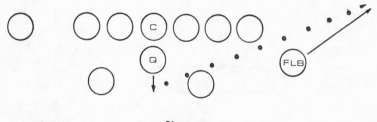

Slant-out

You just ran a slant-in pattern. The play reverses itself and becomes the slant-out when the receiver moves

to the outside. While slants usually net short yardage, a fast and elusive receiver can often turn them into substantial gains.

Many teams vary the slant-in by having the receiver run straight ahead for a few steps before angling inside. Often, you'll see two wide receivers work the slant-in from either side of the line, with the ball then thrown down the middle to the primary receiver.

Down-and-in: Though it achieves much the same purpose, this pattern is the exact opposite of the slant-in. Here, you run not at an angle but straight downfield for a specified number of yards, perhaps fooling your defender into thinking you're going deep. But suddenly you cut sharply and head for the center of the field. Be sure to make a ninety-degree cut. Don't waste time with a curving turn. You must get around fast, for the ball will be delivered at the cut.

Of course, the pattern can be run so that you go on the down-and-out, cutting toward the sideline rather

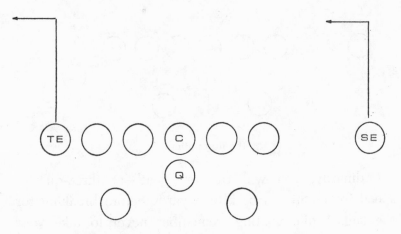

Down-and-out (left) and down-and-in (right)

than the center of the field. The patterns are also
known as the *square-in* and the *square-out*.

Now let's turn to some patterns that promise longer
gains, ones that open the way to the "bomb."

The flag pattern: Your first job on this pattern is to
get past the man covering you. Move off the line
quickly, but travel through the secondary at about
three-quarter speed, keeping your eye on your defender
all the while. Then cut inside, turn again outside, and
streak at full power toward the flag marking the corner
of the end zone. Leave your defender far behind.

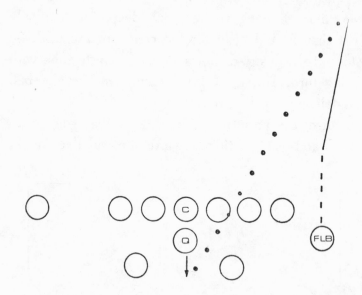

The flag pattern

Ordinarily, you will run—or "float"—at three-quarter
speed for about ten or fifteen yards before breaking for
the flag. While floating, remember never to take your

eyes off your defender; otherwise, you may not be able to protect against some tricky move on his part. The quarterback will pass about three or four seconds after the ball has been snapped. Look for the ball only when you know it is finally in the air.

You may vary the flag pattern in several ways. For instance, the *sideline-flag* pattern sends you out as if you are running the sideline pattern. Make your cut for the sideline, but then turn sharply and head at full power for the flag. The quarterback fakes a throw as you make the cut, after which he resets and fires deep.

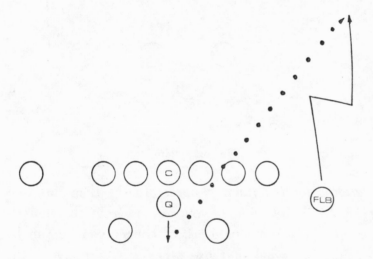

The sideline-flag pattern

The post pattern: You launch this pattern as you do the flag pattern. Move downfield for ten to fifteen yards at about three-quarter speed. Keep your eye on your defender. Then show him your dust, suddenly cutting inside and dashing for the goalpost. Aim right for the middle of the goalpost. Look for the ball once you know it's in the air. The quarterback will need about three or four seconds to unleash the pass.

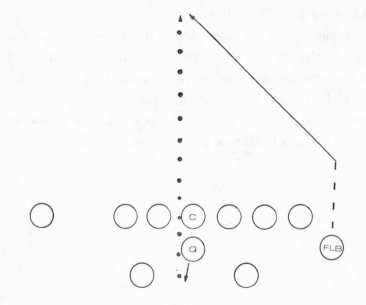

The post pattern

Patterns for the running backs: In the diagrams thus far, you've been running your routes from the flanker-back spot. The same patterns, of course, can be run by the ends. But what of those other prime receivers, the running backs? They, too, can run some of the above patterns, especially if they work from a formation such as the spread set, one that places them up close to the line so that they can burst quickly into the defensive second-ary.

There are, however, a number of patterns designed especially for the running backs. They are seen below for passes thrown to the left. They work equally well to the right.

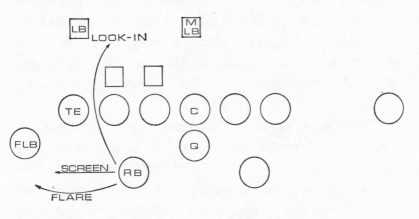

The look-in, screen, and flare patterns

On the *look-in,* you head to the left of your tackle and then swing sharply to the inside, angling away fast from the cornerback. The quarterback drops back a few steps and fires the ball across the line. You should take the ball on stride and continue angling up the field away from the cornerback.

The *screen* is one of the most popular and deceptive of passes. The play opens looking like a run, the whole idea being to draw the defenders in and then pass off to the side. Your tackle and guard first brush-block their men, while you hesitate a moment as if ready to protect the run. Then, as the defenders charge toward the quarterback, you break straight to the outside. In the meantime, your guard and tackle drop back. They join the flankerback and tight end to form a wall—a "screen"—for blocking when the pass comes. The quarterback throws to you. You receive the ball behind the screen and follow your interference into the secondary, leaving the defensive rushers over near the quarterback.

Your pattern for the *flare* is to the outside, just as for the screen. Now, however, do not hesitate, but take off immediately. And run along a curving—a "flaring"— path to the point of reception. And be ready to receive the ball immediately. Most flare passes are in the air for no more than ten yards.

Combination patterns: On many passes, two receivers combine their routes, co-operating to break one of their number free for the reception. One of the most effective of the many combinations is the *ends-cross* pattern. It combines the efforts of the split end and the tight end.

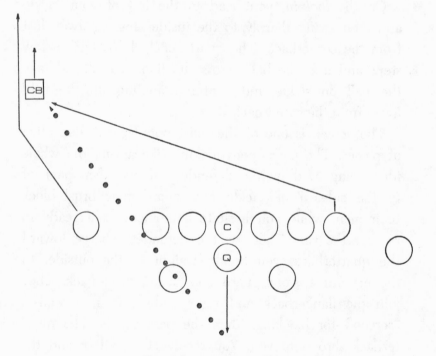

The ends-cross pattern (A)

Let's say that you're the tight end. Far along the line
from you, the split end charges forward at the snap of
the ball. He drives toward the outside of the right cornerback and then streaks downfield, pulling the cornerback with him. In the meantime, *with your eyes constantly on the right cornerback,* you plunge forward a
few steps. As soon as you see him fall back to cover
the split end, you cut at top speed across the secondary, taking the pass in the area that he has vacated.

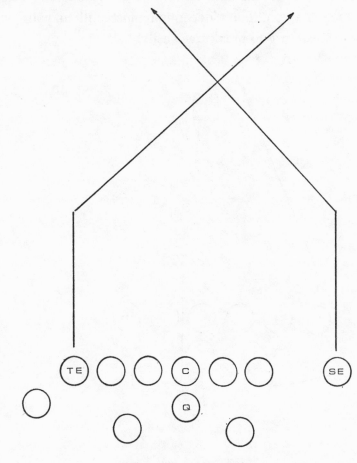

The ends-cross pattern (B)

Teams sometimes vary the ends-cross by sending the ends downfield and then angling them toward each other. The ball goes to the one designated as the primary receiver on the play, or to the man who is better free of his coverage.

The play action pass: The play action pass starts as a running play. Its purpose is to spring you clear for the reception by drawing the defenders in to smother the run. The success of the play depends almost entirely on the abilities of the quarterback and the running backs to fake the run. Their deception must pull in your coverage if you are to break free easily.

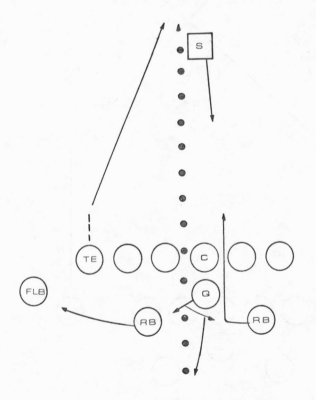

The play action pass

There are many play action passes. In fact, you can execute the pass from practically any running play. Here is an example of how it works.

You're set at the tight end spot. The quarterback takes the ball and first fakes a flip to one running back, who then flares wide. Next, the quarterback fakes the handoff to the second running back. The back rams inside while the quarterback drops back to his passing position, hiding the ball as he moves.

In the meantime, you run at an angle to the middle of the secondary as if readying yourself to block for the back charging inside. Your target appears to be the defensive safety. As the safety moves in for the tackle, you suddenly sprint past him and into the open, ready to take the pass when it comes.

The possibility of the play action pass is an ever-present headache for the men in the defensive secondary. It keeps them from moving in against a run until they are certain the pass is not planned. Their hesitancy strengthens your overall running attack.

Tips

1. When running the sideline and hook patterns, make sure that you receive the ball with at least a yard to spare for the first down.
2. Look for the ball immediately on the slant-in.
3. Make your cuts sharp on the down-and-in and down-and-out patterns.
4. On the post and flag patterns, don't look for the ball until you know it has been thrown.
5. Hesitate before running the screen; don't hesitate at the start of the flare.

5

PASSING AND
RECEIVING

Types of pass: If you play quarterback, you'll throw
two types of forward pass: the drop-back pass and the
running pass. Of the two, you'll attempt the drop-back
far more often, putting it up for short, medium, and
long yardage. The running pass is best used for short
and medium yardage only.

The drop-back pass: This pass takes its name from
the fact that you retreat—drop back—to a given point
behind the line before releasing the ball. For the drop-
back, first make sure that you take the ball with both
hands at the snap and lift it chest high. Then move to
your passing position as quickly as possible. Give the

defense not one extra second in which to cover your receivers or bear down on you.

The backpedal

You're free to drop back in either of two ways. You may backpedal (see Chapters 11 and 14) or, in common with most quarterbacks, turn at the hips and run with a sideways step. The choice is entirely up to you. You should, of course, select whichever method is comfortable and natural, and then practice it until you have it down pat.

The sideways step

As you move back, always look downfield so that you never lose sight of what the defense is doing. Once in position, seek out your primary receiver, but do not look directly at him. Rather, pick up his defender. If you look at the receiver himself, you'll miss the maneuvering of the defender and will be risking a pass that can be easily intercepted or batted away. By watching the defender, you'll see whether he's covering too close for comfort. If so, switch to your secondary receiver.

When you have retreated the proper distance, plant one foot to stop yourself (your right foot if you're right-handed). Then step forward into the pocket and throw. Some passers take one step forward, while others take two. No matter the number of steps, be sure to move forward directly along the line on which you will throw. One foot should be forward at release; it should be the one opposite your throwing arm.

As you step into the pocket, cock the ball behind your ear. Then, as you throw, release your fingers one at a time in the following order: little finger, ring finger, middle finger, thumb, and index finger. The index finger must always be the last to go, for it imparts spin and gives direction to the ball.

Finally, follow through with the throw just as if you are a baseball pitcher. After the ball is away, your arm should be extended at shoulder height. Your palm should be facing the ground. The follow-through gives the ball its final degree of authority and accuracy.

Now, exactly how far back should you drop for the throw? The answer depends on the length of the pass. The long pass needs a deep drop, one that gives the receivers time to move far downfield. The short pass must be thrown quickly and so must come from a shallow drop.

For the short pass, a drop of just three steps is advised. A drop of seven yards is usually required for the medium-range pass. Ten yards is a wise drop for the long pass.

When throwing short, you should deliver the ball within a second and a half after the snap. On both short and medium passes, fire a "clothes line" shot—one that sends the ball traveling fast along a fairly level course; don't "float" or arc the ball, for then it can be easily intercepted or can arrive at the point of reception after the receiver has dashed past.

On long passes, however, put the ball up high, arcing it. A long and level pass gives the defender too much of a chance to cut the ball off.

The running pass: The ball is thrown just as it is on the drop-back. It is cocked behind the ear and released with the usual follow-through. Now, however, it is delivered on the run, and so you need to keep two additional points in mind.

The running pass

First, always try to be running toward the line of scrimmage or toward your receiver as you make the throw. The very momentum of your forward movement will add power and accuracy to the throw.

Second, if you cannot run forward for the pass, then be sure to move in the direction of your throwing arm —to the right if you're right-handed, to the left if you're left-handed. Suppose that you're a right-hander who chooses to travel to the left. To send a pass off to the right, you'll have to twist your body against the momentum of your run. The pass cannot help but be thrown weakly—and, very likely, off target.

The quarterback stance and grip: All-important to the pass is the manner in which you take the ball at the snap. If you take the ball smoothly and correctly, you'll be free to concentrate on the drop-back and the pass. A bobble or an insecure grip can destroy your timing—and the play.

On breaking huddle, set yourself directly behind the center, with your feet a shoulder width apart and parallel to each other. Flex your knees, making yourself comfortable. Position your hands beneath the center. Let the heels of your palms touch each other. Spread your fingers, but keep them relaxed so that they'll close quickly and easily about the ball.

At the snap, take the ball in its "fat" part. The ball should come to you in a way that permits the fingers of your throwing hand to close over the lacing. The fingers will then be securely "locked" to the ball for the pass. Should they not be located exactly to your liking, turn the ball to the correct position as you drop back.

The stance and grip described here are also used for the run. Again, take the ball in its fat part, with your fingers over the laces for a secure hold. Now, however, there is one difference. On the pass, you hold the ball up near your shoulders. For the run or the handoff, bring the ball close to your stomach. It will then be low enough for the handoff or for a quick shift to your carrying arm.

Incidentally, whether planning a pass or a run, call your signals at the line in a clear voice. Use a staccato count that will help your teammates develop a sense of rhythm so that they can move out, swiftly and together, at the snap. Throughout the count, keep your eyes on the defense.

Now let's move you out of the quarterback spot and take a look at the other side of the pass—the reception.

Rules for receivers: If you're to be a successful receiver, you will always need to keep six basic rules uppermost in mind. Together, they give you the best chance of completing the majority of passes thrown your way. Here they are now:

1. Run your exact route, always arriving at the point of reception at the expected time. You may vary the route slightly on any play to avoid or confuse your defender, but make certain that you're always where you're supposed to be when the ball is thrown. The quarterback will search out your defender and then pass to your assigned area. You must be there for the catch.

2. No matter the length of the pass, do not look for the ball too soon as you run your route. Rather, watch the defenders around you. Work to outrun them so that you have the clearest field possible for the reception.

But how—without eyes in the back of your head—can you know exactly when the ball is delivered? The best answer is the count system. With your quarterback, work out a count for each pass—say, a count of four for one pass, a count of five for another. Then, as you head downfield, say the count to yourself. After the final number, look back. The ball should be coming to you.

3. Once you do look at the ball, however, never take your eyes off of it. Literally, as all good receivers do, "look it into your hands." Avoid all temptation to glance at your defender or at the open territory that may lie between you and the end zone. The merest glance away will destroy the co-ordination that must exist between your hands and eyes. Your hands will move to the wrong spot. Or the ball will be closer than expected when you again look back. In either case, you'll be in deep trouble.

4. Wait until the ball is approaching before raising your arms to take it. Never run your route with your arms upraised. You'll only slow yourself and throw yourself off balance. Rather, carry your arms just as you would if running down the street, using them for balance and to pump speed into your dash. Then send them up as the ball is coming down.

5. Keep your hands relaxed and slightly cupped for the catch. If tensed, they will be unable to close

quickly and easily about the ball. And, if tensed, the ball will treat them as if they are a brick wall. It will hit them and bounce away.

The fact is that you should keep your *entire body* relaxed for the catch. Be eager to make the reception, but not too eager. Do not jump for the ball too soon; you'll only come back down ahead of time, leaving your defender still up there for the interception. Do not start to run for the end zone before you have the ball firmly in hand; you'll bobble the catch or sprint "right out from under the ball." Once you've completed the reception, pull the ball against your body. Look for daylight. Protect against the fumble if you're hit quickly.

6. Watch out for *offensive* pass interference. Just as the receiver may not interfere with your right to catch the ball, you may not interfere with his right to intercept or bat it away. So do all that you can to make the catch, but do not keep him from doing his job by pushing, bumping, or grabbing him. To avoid the penalty levied for offensive pass interference, you need to memorize one rule: *Always play the ball, not the man.*

Tips

1. When dropping back to pass, look downfield, first picking out the defender covering your primary receiver; if the primary receiver is too closely covered, switch to your secondary receiver.

2. As you pass, let your index finger be the last one to leave the ball; the index finger gives the ball

spin and direction. Always follow through on your throw as if you are a baseball pitcher.

3. When throwing on the run, try to be moving toward the line of scrimmage or your target as you release the ball; your forward momentum will add power and accuracy to the pass.

4. Learn the correct quarterback stance and grip so that you'll be able to take the ball smoothly for either the pass or the run.

5. Memorize and put to use the basic rules for pass receivers, always remembering to wait until the ball is in the air before looking back for it and always trying to make the catch with your whole body relaxed.

6. To avoid a penalty for offensive pass interference, always play the ball, not the man.

6

THE KICKING GAME

Kicks: Along with the run and the pass, the kick is a basic offensive weapon. Punts carry you out of danger after you've failed to make a first down. Field goals and kicks for points-after-touchdown net extra tallies that often mean the difference between defeat and victory. Kickoff returns are aimed at giving you the best field position possible; sometimes they produce that most exciting play of all, the dash along the full length of the field to a touchdown.

The purpose of this chapter and the next is to look at the kicking game from the standpoint of both the kicker and the receiver. We'll start with the kicker and that first play of every game: the kickoff.

Kicking off: The kicker has much freedom in deciding how he wishes to handle the kickoff. For instance, he has the choice of setting the ball on a tee, propping it up in a hole that he's made in the turf with his heel, or placing it flat on the ground. Next, he can choose how far he'll run on the approach to the kick; the average approach covers about seven yards or so, but he may run a shorter or longer distance if he feels that either will give him greater momentum. Finally, he may kick the ball in either of two ways: *straight-on* or *soccer style*.

As a kicker, you must consider all these choices carefully. Settle on the ones most comfortable for you. Only when you're comfortable will you have the chance of getting off a good kick—one of those sixty-yarders that enables your men to smother the receiver before he gets to the twenty-yard marker.

As the name suggests, you come straight at the ball for the straight-on kickoff. Run slowly and keep your eye on the ball, taking aim on the spot where you wish to make contact. Your nonkicking foot should arrive just behind and to the side of the ball. Your kicking toe should strike the ball just below midpoint, with your kicking leg locking just as you make contact. Swing your leg up as if it were a pendulum. Follow the pendulum swing through to its very end.

If kicked correctly, the ball should ride high and come down deep, traveling end-over-end. Without sacrificing distance, always put the ball up as high as you can. Then your men will have ample time to close in on the receiver.

For the soccer style kick, you approach the ball on a

The straight-on kickoff

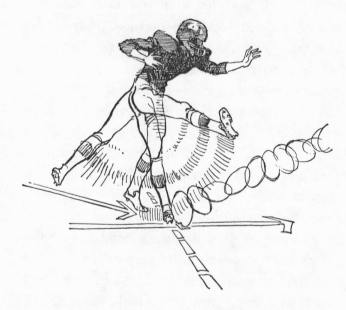

The soccer style kickoff

diagonal—usually at about a forty-five-degree angle. Again, run the distance of your choice, but this time swing your leg so that you strike the ball not with your toe but with the top of your foot—your instep. And, again, keep your eye on the ball as you approach, take aim, and follow your leg swing through to the end.

Whether kicking straight-on or soccer style, you should first aim for height and accuracy. In particular, make the ball go where you want it to go. Power will come with practice.

The on-side kickoff: The on-side kickoff is usually seen late in a tight game. Let's say that, with just a minute left in the final quarter, your team has scored, but still needs another touchdown for the win. Your coach knows that, once you've kicked off, you'll not likely regain possession before time runs out. He calls for the on-side kickoff.

This bit of strategy takes advantage of a certain rule governing kickoffs. The rule states that, once the ball is touched by any defensive player, it becomes a free ball. Until the whistle blows, the ball belongs to any man who can get his hands on it, including any man on the kicking team. And so the whole idea is to send the ball ten yards or so to the front wall of the receiving team. Then, hopefully, one of your men will be able to snatch the ball up in the melee that always follows the kick.

But there's a snag. The ball must not only be kicked short, it must also be kicked along the ground. If you loft it into the air, the receiver will be able to kill the strategy by signaling for a fair catch and thus ending the play.

For the on-side kickoff, make your approach as usual. Now, however, aim for a spot somewhat above the midpoint on the ball. By striking the ball high, you will drive it downward and send it skittering along the ground. Put enough power into the kick to get the needed ten yards. Then cross your fingers.

Punting: Now let's change the game situation. Let's say that it's fourth down, with six yards to go for the first down. The coach sends you in to punt the ball away.

Take your position a safe distance behind the center (pro kickers stand fifteen yards back, but you may need to come in closer to be within the range of the center's snap). Stand there relaxed, with your knees flexed and your body bent slightly forward from the hips. Extend your arms, holding your elbows close to your sides and setting your hands about waist high. Your palms, offering the center a target, should be facing inward and downward. Your fingers should be extended forward.

Keep your eye on the ball as it comes to you and receive it with *both* hands. If you glance up to see what the defense is doing, you're in danger of missing or bobbling the catch. And if you try to "grandstand" it with a one-handed catch—well, you know the disaster and embarrassment you're courting.

As do most punters, you'll probably use a two-step or a three-step approach. Let's say that you prefer the two-step. While you wait for the snap, your kicking foot is slightly to the front. Now, with the ball in your

The punt

hands, you move forward on your kicking foot, taking a short step. Follow with a natural step on your nonkicking foot and then swing your kicking leg up to the ball. On the step with your nonkicking foot, release the ball, letting it drop to meet the kick. Throughout the approach and the kicking swing, keep your eyes on the ball.

The ball should be dropped from a little below waist level. Too much can go wrong—and too much time can be lost—if the ball is released from, say, shoulder or head height.

For the three-step approach, you stand with your nonkicking foot forward and then step out on it. You continue with a step on your kicking foot and another on your nonkicking foot. Then you swing into the kick.

Whether you use the two- or three-step approach, adjust the ball as you walk forward. Turn the lacings upward so that the ball presents a smooth surface for the kick. Hold the ball at a slight downward slant to its front, and at about a fifteen-degree angle along its long axis. The angle will help provide spiral, which gives the ball distance by enabling it to cut easily through the air.

To contribute further to that spiral, you should strike the ball at a point slightly on the side of your foot. Your foot should meet the ball just above knee level. Lock your leg and follow through all the way on the kicking action, carrying your kicking foot above your head.

You want your punts to travel high, deep, and on target. As with the kickoff, look first for height and accuracy. You'll acquire power with practice.

Place kicking: Now for another change in game situation. Your team has just scored or has come close enough for a field goal. In you go to see if your "magic toe" can put some additional points on the scoreboard.

With your kicking foot slightly forward and your arms relaxed at your sides, take your position about a step and a half behind the holder. The holder kneels about seven yards to the rear of the center. When you're ready to kick, tell the holder. He'll then signal the center for the snap.

When the holder receives the ball and holds it

angled against the ground in front of you, move forward a half step on your kicking foot, following it with a longer, natural step on your nonkicking foot, after which your kicking foot comes forward to the ball. All the while, keep your head down and your eyes on the ball, aiming for the spot where you want to make contact. In the instant of impact, lock your ankle. By making a single unit of your ankle and foot, this "locking" adds power and accuracy to the kick.

The place kick

Follow through with your swing. Continue to keep your head down. Continue to look at the spot you were aiming for on the ball, even though the ball has now disappeared from view. If you look up to see where the ball is traveling, you'll ruin your follow-through and likely send the ball off course.

On short place kicks, aim to strike the ball just below the midpoint so that you'll give it good height. Aim a little higher on the ball for longer kicks. The ball will travel somewhat lower but will pick up additional distance.

Now it's time to shift you from the kicker's spot over to that of the receiver. We'll begin the next chapter with the kickoff and set you for the deep reception.

Tips

1. On every kind of kick, keep your eyes on the ball.
2. Likewise, always follow through with your kicking action.
3. On kickoffs and punts, lock your leg as your foot makes contact with the ball.
4. On place kicks, lock your ankle as your foot meets the ball.
5. When learning to kick, aim first for accuracy and height. Power will come with practice.

7

RECEIVING KICKS

Kickoff returns: You and your fellow deep receiver station yourselves at or near the goal line (you should stand out far enough to be sure that you're within the kicker's range). Up ahead, your teammates are divided into two lines extending across the field. In the far distance, five men form the front wall. Closer to you are four men, known collectively as the "wedge."

You see the kicker move forward. The ball comes arcing through the air to you. You must now do three things:

First, no matter what happens, *field the ball safely.* Once it is touched by the receiving team, the ball is declared free. Should you drop it, it may then be picked up by any opponent, with possession then going to his team.

Even if it rolls into the end zone, you may not leave it untended, for it then could mean a loss of six points. So get to it fast.

Second, keep your eyes on the ball throughout its flight. Some beginners worry about the approaching defenders and spend half the time watching them. The usual result is a missed or bobbled catch. Actually, on a kickoff, there's no reason to be concerned about the defenders. They have a long ways to run and will likely still be yards away when you take the ball.

Third, keep the ball in front of you. Back up if it's sailing beyond you. Step to one side or the other as necessary. In all, never have your back to the defenders when the ball comes down, and never let it hit the ground. You'll lose too much time getting turned around—and much too much time chasing after a ball that is bouncing over the turf.

All right. Let's say that you're in perfect position. The ball is dropping right into your arms. Avoid the temptation to reach up and grab it with your hands. Rather, make a cradle of your arms, wait for the ball to drop against your midsection, and then fold your cradled arms about it.

Throughout, remain relaxed. Keep yourself from running until you've completed the catch. Tense muscles or a premature move forward can easily pop the ball right out of your grasp.

Once you've made the catch, you may move in one of three directions: straight ahead or to either side. The direction will be determined in the huddle before the kickoff. Take off in that direction now, moving fast and *immediately looking for the men in the wedge.* Their job is to block out the defenders charging downfield. As soon as you see a wedgeman ahead of you take out or knock a defender aside, head through the hole he has made and accelerate to full power.

You must run fast from the moment you take the ball, your aim being to get as close to the wedge as possible so that you can quickly take advantage of any opening. Under no circumstances, however, are you to "hot dog" it by outrunning the wedge before a path has been cleared for you. Let the blockers do their part. They'll add precious yards to your run—and may even spring you free for a dash to the goal line.

Once you're through the hole, accelerate fast. Good kickoff returns depend almost entirely on speed.

Punt returns: You field the punt just as you do the kickoff. Maneuver so that the ball is always to your front, allow it to drop against your midsection, and then fold your cradled arms about it. Never take your eyes off the ball until the catch is made. Remain relaxed throughout.

The punt reception is far more dangerous than the kickoff reception, for now the defenders are playing much closer to you. Still, keep your eyes on the ball. Then, no matter whether you're receiving short or deep, head for daylight, perhaps aiming to the outside and then cutting back in as the defenders flow over to the outside. All the while, try to pick up some interference. If you're playing deep, look for the short receiver. He may be able to throw a key block for you.

Make every effort to catch the punted ball. But if a

catch proves impossible, stay clear of the ball once it
hits the ground. Should the ball touch you in any way
—even nick you—it will be regarded as a fumble. It will
belong to the opposition if a defender then manages to
grab it. And, since the area will be full of charging de-

The fair catch—right

fenders, the chances of a recovery are all in their favor. For this reason, never deliberately allow the ball to hit the ground so that it can be taken on the bounce. Always pick it out of the air.

The fair catch: When receiving a kick, you are entitled to raise your arm in the fair catch signal. The signal, which is given when the defenders have come too close for comfort while the ball is yet in the air, ena-

The fair catch—wrong

bles you to field the ball without being touched by them. Once you have caught the ball, you then may not run with it.

Because you must keep your eyes on the approaching ball, you'll have to sense rather than actually see the defenders. As you plant yourself for the catch, have your arm ready for the signal. Should you then think that you'll be tackled immediately, raise your arm. If not, take the ball and start looking for daylight.

One point must always be remembered about the signal. You must always extend your arm to its *full length* so that there will be no doubt that you're calling for the fair catch. Should you raise your arm just slightly—or raise both arms as if readying yourself for the catch—your team will be penalized fifteen yards from the point of the infraction.

Tips

1. On every kick reception, keep the ball in front of you, let it drop against your midsection, and then fold your cradled arms about it.
2. Always field kickoffs and then quickly run up close behind the wedge, looking for the first hole that opens.
3. Try never to let a punted ball touch the ground; if it does, stay away from it.
4. Always raise your arm to its full length when calling for the fair catch.

8

PROTECTING YOUR MAN

Blocking: No matter how brilliantly conceived a play may be, it will fail unless the man with the ball is protected from the tacklers. Blocking provides that protection. It is the football art of slamming into an opponent and using your shoulders and body—but *never* your hands —to keep him from reaching the carrier. It is an art that every man on the team must learn.

If you are a lineman, blocking is your main assignment; and if you are the quarterback or a running back, the coach will expect you to block—and block expertly—whenever you are not actually handling the ball. Additionally, whether you be a lineman or a back, he will insist that you know several types of block.

The shoulder block: This is the block that you'll most often use as a lineman. Its purpose is to clear a path for the carrier on running plays. With it, you drive the defender straight back or to one side or the other. The direction depends on the play. The whole idea is to move the defender in a direction opposite that of the play—to the left, for instance, if the carrier is to ram past on your right.

Once you come up to the line from the huddle, drop into the three-point stance, which was described in Chapter 3. Know the direction in which you intend to move the defender, but give him no clue as to what you have in mind. Do not obviously shift your weight to one side or the other, nor shove one shoulder forward. Above all, do not let your eyes give you away with nervous glances. Square yourself to the line and look straight ahead, right at the defender, keeping your face a blank.

On the snap, plunge forward, fast and hard. Make contact with your shoulder and the side of your neck. Turn your head to the side and churn your feet, driving them hard against the turf. No matter what the defender attempts in an effort to cast you aside—the head slap or the grab-and-shake, for instance—do not lose contact with him. Continue to drive him back or to the side.

The head-up block: Let's move into the backfield and try a block used there for pass protection.

Playing the running back spot, you take a crouching stance, with your feet comfortably apart and your body

The shoulder block (A)

The shoulder block (B)

bent forward from the hips. Let your arms curve down in front of your legs. Close your hands into fists. Keep your head up so that you can watch the defense. Make certain that you are perfectly balanced.

The play breaks and a lineman rushes at you. Remain crouched, but don't allow him to come all the way to you, for then he will have gathered enough momentum to knock you over. Rather, move forward to meet him, rising slightly out of the crouch and bringing your arms and hands across your chest. Meet him solidly with your shoulders thrusting forward. Drive him back, but do not do so by pushing him with your hands. A hand push is illegal and will net you a penalty.

At no time before or during the block should you draw back. If you retreat, you can all too easily be swept aside or bowled over. And, throughout, remain on your feet. Never make the mistake of flinging yourself at the defender's ankles. You won't topple him as planned. If he has an ounce of agility—and the biggest of defensive men are surprisingly agile—he'll simply jump over you.

The cross-body block: The cross-body block, which is often simply called the body block, is usually put to use in open-field situations. Perhaps, as you're running interference for a carrier who has moved deep into the secondary and is about to break clear, you see the safety closing in. Prepare yourself for the cross-body block.

When the safety is within range, throw your body across his upper legs. On impact, snap hard against him, using your hips and upper legs to provide the

The cross-body block

power that will drive him back. Unless absolutely necessary, do not leave the ground and dive across the tackler. Once you've hit the man, you want to remain right with him so that you can continue applying the pressure. A dive, even though on target, will likely carry you past the tackler and put an end to the block.

All is well and fine if you knock the man off his feet. But it is not necessary to do so. Your whole purpose is to delay him long enough to enable the carrier to charge past. But delay the tackler as long as possible. If he doesn't go down, continue to push against him, "crab-walking" him back by pressing your hands against the ground and arching your back as high as possible.

Two points of caution: As on any block, do not use

your hands on the defender; he is permitted to grab your jersey or thrust you aside with his hands, but you are not allowed to reply in kind without incurring a penalty. Second, be sure that you always block the man from the front or the side. Should you hit him from behind, you'll be penalized fifteen yards for clipping. Accidental clips occur from time to time, but do all that you can to keep your record free of them.

Backfield men also employ the cross-body block on plays close to the line of scrimmage. In similar situations, you may need to throw:

The drive block: This is the simplest of blocks. As you approach the defender, run at him and drive your head into him, either knocking him down or aside. For best results, you'd best hit him from a crouched position. Keep your head up throughout so that you can take aim on the man and compensate for any evasive moves on his part.

Blocking for kicks and passes: Line blocking for kicks and passes differs from that for runs. When blocking for the run, you must drive your man back or to the side. For the kick and pass, however, you rise out of your stance to a crouch, take the rush, and then stand firm against it, preventing the tackler from getting around you.

To protect the kicker, stand still once you have come up from the stance. Meet the rusher and hit back, but don't surrender a single backward step and, unless absolutely necessary to keep him to your front, don't move to either side. Remain where you are, in close contact with your fellow linemen, forming a solid wall that holds the rush at bay until the kick is safely away.

When protecting the passer, rise to a crouch and take a backward step to join in forming the pocket. Then meet your defender with a series of jabbing blocks. Recover quickly after each one and immediately throw another. Always keep your man to your front. This can be done by staying in close to him, moving in whatever direction he takes, and continuing with the jabbing blocks.

The basics of blocking: Five fundamental rules govern good blocking. They help guarantee that your every block, no matter what type it may be, will always be a good one. They should be memorized before the first day of practice and then remembered throughout the season. They are:

1. Always have the firmest footing possible on every block. Insecure footing weakens the block by preventing you from carrying all the way through against the defender.

2. Keep your eyes open on every block, taking careful aim on the defender and compensating for his every evasive move.

3. Aim "through" the defender to a point beyond him. This will help you to follow through with the block. Otherwise, you may simply graze the man, miss him altogether, or be pushed aside.

4. Set up your block so that your body is always between the defender and the carrier. Always move the tackler away from the carrier's path.

5. Get under the tackler so that you have maximum leverage. You'll then find it easier to push him back, especially if you hit him low enough to lift him off his feet.

Tips

1. Prior to the start of the play, never let the defender know the direction in which you plan to take him with the shoulder block.
2. On the head-up block, never let the defender come all the way to you; step forward to meet him.
3. On the cross-body block, hit the defender across the upper legs; if you don't knock him off his feet, continue with the block by "crab-walking" him away from the carrier.
4. On the drive block, meet your man in a crouched position.
5. Rise to a crouch and stand still when protecting the kicker; move back a step to help form the pocket when protecting the passer. In both cases, keep your defender to your front.
6. Memorize the basics of good blocking, remember them, and apply them.

Defensive Strategy

9

STOP THAT PLAY!

Defensive alignments: As any linebacker will tell you, there are as many defensive alignments in football today as there are offensive formations. Their purpose, of course, is exactly opposite that of the formation. With the formation, the offense triggers the play in the best way possible. With the alignment, the defense digs in to stop the play dead in its tracks.

All good defensive alignments share one characteristic in common: They provide adequate coverage against both the pass and the run. Some put more pressure on one than the other. Some can be varied to intensify the pressure on one or the other. But not one leaves the pass uncovered, and not one ignores the run. Only by covering both can you hope to stop the welter of plays that will be thrown at you.

In this chapter, we'll look at some of today's most effective basic alignments, and then move on to two that are reserved for special game situations. But first a word of general explanation:

The number system: When first learning the alignments, you'll find that most are identified by a series of numbers. The numbers in any series always total eleven, equaling the number of men in the unit. Don't let the numbers confuse you, for they simply indicate the locations of all the players in the alignment.

For instance, a football veteran of many years is the 6-2-2-1 defense. The numbers indicate that there are six men on the line. Behind them are two linebackers, two cornerbacks, and a single safety.

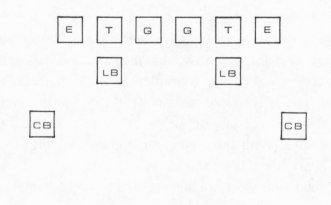

The 6-2-2-1 defense

Incidentally, though it was once a popular alignment, the 6-2-2-1 is no longer much used. The reason: The two cornerbacks and the single safety are really too few for the pass. Another man is needed. The best pass defense is to be had in alignments calling for two cornerbacks and two safeties.

For instance:

The 4-3-2-2 defense: With a second safety in the secondary and seven men up guarding the line, this formation divides its attention pretty equally between the pass and the run. For the sake of convenience, it is usually called the 4-3, with the numbers referring to the linemen and the linebackers. Without needing to say so, football men know that two cornerbacks and two safeties are always used in the alignment. At times, you'll hear the setup called the 4-3-4.

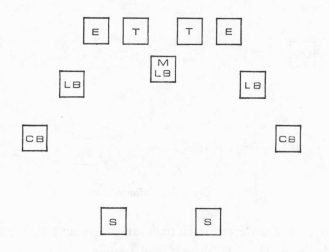

The 4-3-2-2 defense

The linemen, of course, are responsible for stopping the run or getting to the quarterback before he can pass. The linebackers first watch for passes fired just over the line and then, should a run develop, join the linemen for the tackle. The cornerbacks and the safeties have one main target: the pass receivers. The cornerbacks are also charged with bringing down the runner should he burst through the line and make his way to their area.

Simple adjustments of the 4-3 will give you such alignments as the 5-2-4, which puts five men directly on the line and sets two linebackers behind them. The alignment adds a degree of pressure to one side of the line or the other, while still leaving four men back to defend against the pass.

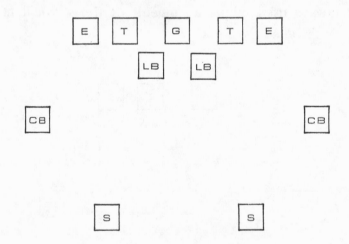

The 5-2-4 defense

The 6-1-2-2 defense: Here is an alignment that uses a single linebacker. With just one player at the linebacker spot, six men are able to work right on the line and thus increase the pressure on the run. Adequate pass coverage continues with the two cornerbacks and the two safeties. The linebacker adds to the run protection by being free to move to any point on the line where he is needed.

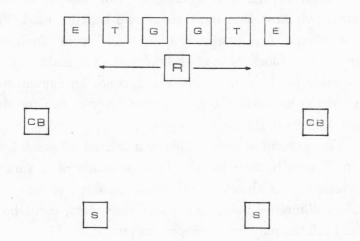

The 6-1-2-2 defense

The alignment is particularly effective against the run if your linebacker is very strong, very tough, and very fast—ideally, the most aggressive man on defense. He must quickly sight the run, move fast to the spot where he is needed, and then pitch in hard to help bring down the carrier. Because he is free to move all along the line, he was long ago named the "rover." But because he must be so aggressive, he has come to be better known as the "monster man." In fact, some coaches now refer to the 6-1-2-2 as the "monster defense."

The monster man often positions himself at the center of the line so that he can move to one side or the other with equal ease. Quite often, however, he works the wide side of the field. Statistics show that most long runs are made to the wide side, and so he stations himself there to add another defender in the expected direction of the run.

Tough though it is against the run, the 6-1-2-2 contains two flaws that must always be kept in mind. First, the offense can easily "double team" your linebacker, using two blockers against him and thus making it impossible for him to do his job. Second, he cannot cover short passes across the line as effectively as can the three linebackers in the 4-3 alignment.

The prevent defense: This is a special alignment that you'll usually save for the final moments of a game in which you're ahead. It is similar to the 4-3 setup, the chief difference being that your linebackers, cornerbacks, and safeties play much deeper than usual.

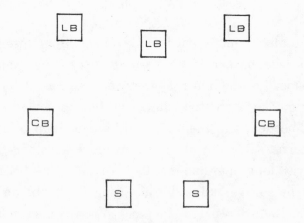

The prevent defense

You know that the offense must go for the long gain if it is to score, and the whole strategy here is to protect against the "bomb" that can put six points on the board. With just four men on the line and the linebackers deep, you're going to give up yardage on short runs and short passes. But there's nothing to worry about as long as you make certain they *stay short*. Stifle the long gain, and the clock will do the rest.

The goal line defense: As its name indicates, this alignment is used when your back is up against your own end zone. All your men move up close to the line, the main idea being to protect against the run. In the following formation—just one of several possible—six men are on the line, with the linebackers right behind them. The safeties, also up close, play wide to protect against the short pass or the sweep. As soon as they see an inside run developing, they join the scramble to reach the carrier.

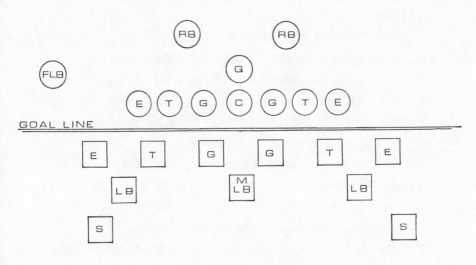

The goal line defense

Heads-up defense: When assigned to the defensive unit, your job is the same as that of any offensive man: You must learn your team's every defensive alignment and know your place in each. Then, from the moment that you begin to practice, play heads-up ball, staying alert from start to finish. At times, defensive alignments must be quickly rearranged when you sense that you've guessed wrong as to the coming play—when, for instance, you're set for a run and then pick up a clue that a pass is in the offing. Listen closely for the signals calling for the defensive change, then make your adjustment quickly and confidently. Be ready to carry out your assignment, immediately and aggressively, when the play breaks.

Tips

1. Remember always that the best defensive alignments provide good coverage against both the pass and the run.
2. When using the 6-1-2-2 defense, always set your most aggressive man at the linebacker spot.
3. When you're ahead with minutes left, bring out your prevent defense. Protect against the "bomb" that can net the offense six points. Instead, give up short yardage while the clock runs out.
4. Learn your team's every defensive alignment and know where you play in each.
5. Stay alert for signals calling for a change in any alignment. Readjust yourself quickly.
6. Be ready to carry out your assignment, immediately and aggressively, as soon as the play breaks.

10

PASS DEFENSE

Three basic defenses: There are three basic types of pass defense: *man-to-man,* the *zone,* and the *blitz.* Man-to-man and zone coverage are general defenses. The blitz is used occasionally or in special game situations.

Your team may put the emphasis on just one of the general defenses, employing it most of the time. You will, however, need to master all three, for each will be needed at one point or another in a game. For instance, though the zone may be your primary defense, you'll want to switch to man-to-man when the opposition moves close to your end zone. The zone is more vulnerable to the short pass than is man-to-man coverage, yielding a bit of yardage that you can ill afford when deep in your own territory.

The purpose of this chapter is to look at the three defenses in turn. In the next chapter, we'll talk about how
best to handle each.

Man-to-man coverage: As its name indicates, man-to-
man coverage assigns each linebacker and each defensive back (a cornerback or safety) to a given receiver.
The linebackers are usually charged with covering the
offensive backs and are especially watchful for the short
pass. The defensive backs, alert for anything from a
short pass to the bomb, are customarily assigned as follows:

The cornerbacks handle the split end and the flankerback, both of whom are deep receivers. The free safety
assists the cornerback on his side of the secondary. The
strong safety covers the tight end. (The strong safety,
by the way, is not named for his physical strength; the
name comes from the fact that he plays over on what is
called the strong side of the offensive line—the side on
which the tight end is stationed.)

When the ball is snapped, each defender moves with
his receiver, making certain that he never allows his man
to get behind him and into the clear for the reception.
As soon as the pass is thrown, the defender plays the
ball. If it is thrown to a receiver other than his own, he
leaves his man immediately and moves in the direction
of the pass so that he can assist his teammates in the
tackle.

Zone coverage: Zone coverage is a relatively new type
of defense, but it is becoming increasingly popular as
the years go by, especially in the professional ranks.

Now, instead of being assigned individual receivers, the linebackers and the defensive backs are each given certain areas to protect. On the snap, each moves to his area and covers any receiver who comes running into it.

Zone defenses vary somewhat from team to team, and, particularly, from play to play, with these latter variations much depending on the offense's actions. Your coach will determine the zones for your unit and will instruct you as to how they are to be played in given game situations. In general, however, the linebackers handle the short zones; these zones range back from the line for about ten yards or so. The cornerbacks play the deep zones, zones that pick up where those of the linebackers stop; they extend all the way to the goal line. The free safety works the center of the field, and the strong safety joins the cornerback in the deep zone on the strong side of the offensive line.

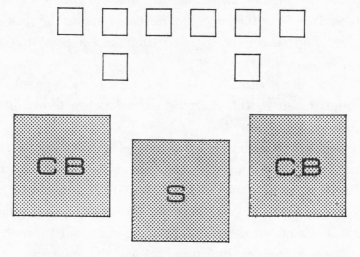

The zones

With the snap of the ball, each defender moves quickly to his area. He keeps his man in front of him. Then he plays the ball, sprinting to the area where it is thrown.

The rush of the linemen is all-important in the zone defense. They must not give the quarterback a substantial amount of time for the throw. Why? When playing the zone, you'll be able to maintain your position in the zone with ease for about a count of five after the play breaks. But as the time stretches out, you'll experience difficulty in maintaining your position and covering the receiver.

The blitz: The blitz is reserved for those times when you're certain that the offense is going to pass. The tactic, which is also known as the "red dog," sends the linemen and linebackers charging directly at the quarterback. They move as fast as possible and are sometimes joined by one or two defensive backs. The whole purpose is to smother the quarterback before he has the chance to throw, or to hurry him into a pass that will fall off-target.

The blitz is often worked from the 4-3 alignment. The routes taken by the charging defenders are shown in the following diagram.

The blitz can be an awesome defensive weapon, leading to a quarterback sack and a substantial loss of yards. But it must be played with care, with the whole maneuver called off if you think the quarterback is signaling for a change to the run. The hard rush will prevent the defenders from pulling up short and downing the carrier should the pass be replaced with, say, a draw or a trap.

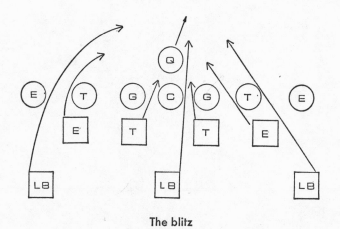

The blitz

Tips

1. Know the three basic pass defenses.

2. On man-to-man coverage, move with your receiver and then play the ball when it is thrown, leaving your man if the pass is aimed elsewhere.

3. On zone coverage, move immediately to your area of responsibility; then play the ball, running to wherever it is thrown.

4. Remember, the rush is all-important to the zone defense; give the quarterback little time to throw so that the defender will be able to maintain his position in the zone and cover the receiver.

5. Use the blitz with care; it can be a fine defensive weapon, but a runner can also quickly slip past while the quarterback is being charged.

11

THE TACTICS OF
PASS COVERAGE

Covering man-to-man: To see how best to cover the pass man-to-man, let's play you first as a defensive back. When you take your place in the alignment, immediately look through your receiver to the ball. Your eyes must be on the ball when it is snapped. Then you'll waste no time in moving into your covering pattern.

As soon as the play breaks, begin to move backward. Do not turn and run toward your man, but backpedal your way over in front of him. In this way, you'll keep him in front of you and keep the quarterback in full view. You'll see the pass thrown. And, beforehand, the quarterback may give you a clue as to its intended target by unintentionally looking in the direction of the throw.

When backpedaling, use short, shuffling steps. Carry your weight forward on your feet so that you don't lose your balance and topple backward. Move your feet alongside each other, ignoring any temptation to gain speed by crossing one leg in front of the other. With the cross step, you can all too easily trip yourself.

Above all, keep your man in front of you. For the defensive back, there's nothing more embarrassing than to have the receiver suddenly dash past, move into the clear, and take the pass for a touchdown. To protect against an unexpected sprint, maintain a distance of about three yards between yourself and the receiver. Those few yards will give you the reaction time necessary to cover any sudden moves on his part.

Backpedal for as long as needs be and then break downfield with the receiver, running alongside him, and staying in close. But play the ball, not the man. If the ball comes your way, go after it, batting it away or—if the circumstances are right—intercepting it. But should the pass go to another man, leave your receiver immediately. Get to the ball fast and lend a hand with the tackle.

Now let's switch you to the linebacker spot and see what must be done there. On the snap, delay your man as he comes at you, giving him a shove or jamming him with your hands and arms. Do whatever you can to slow him down or knock him off stride. Should he get past you, do no more shoving. Otherwise you'll be penalized for pass interference.

When moving to the receiver, backpedal. Do not immediately turn and run with him. For all you know, a play other than a pass to your man may be in the offing. If turned away from the quarterback, you won't see it develop. And you won't be able to swing around and move in quickly for the stop. Backpedal until you see that your man is committed to moving downfield. Then turn and run with him. Most times, you will not backpedal more than five yards.

Finally, as does the defensive back, play the ball rather than the man. Move to wherever it is thrown.

Covering the zone: Whether playing as a defensive back or a linebacker, backpedal immediately to your area of responsibility. Just as when playing man-to-man, keep in front of any man who enters your area. Watch the quarterback so that you never lose sight of the play that might develop. React to the ball as soon as it is thrown. Move directly to it.

Covering on the blitz: If you're a defensive back, the responsibility for pass coverage will fall to you, for the linebackers will be involved in the rush to the quarterback. Move up close to your receiver, setting yourself perhaps five to seven yards away. Then move to him fast. Expect the pass immediately. Under hard pressure, the quarterback probably won't hold the ball for more than a second or so.

Bump-and-run: A constant headache for any pass defender is the fact that receivers are fast and fleet. If given the chance, they can easily outrun practically any defensive man in football. A weapon that slows them down is the bump-and-run.

When planning the bump-and-run, line up close to your receiver, either straight in front of him or a shade toward his inside shoulder. Then move forward with the snap of the ball and hit the man. As he comes to you, take him with your shoulder or with your arms up at chest level. Aim to stop him cold, slow him down, or knock him off balance.

When the receiver manages to break free, turn and run downfield with him. Run alongside and match him stride for stride, but do not bump him again if you first hit him when he was three yards beyond the line of scrimmage. A recent rule change states that only one bump is allowed beyond that point. Also, the rules now prevent you from taking the receiver out of the play with a block below the waist.

As you run, keep your eyes on the receiver. Do not look back for the ball until he does so. Should you glance back earlier, you'll lose speed and enable him to race ahead.

The interception: The dream of all pass defenders is to intercept the pass and then carry the ball all the way back upfield to the touchdown.

As a defender, you'll have your fair share of opportunities for the interception. But don't be tempted by it every time the ball sails in your direction. Attempted interceptions on *every* pass lead to fatal mistakes. Learn to determine whether the oncoming ball is best caught or batted away. Experience will teach you how to do this.

Two points should always be kept in mind:

First, don't ever allow your receiver to get behind you while you are deciding whether to intercept the pass. If you miss and he then makes the catch, you'll be left standing flat-footed. It's better to bat the ball down than to give the receiver the opportunity of getting into the open.

Second, when you do decide to go for the interception, leap high for the ball. Always try to catch it at its highest point as it is descending. A high leap will put you above the receiver and make the catch all the easier.

Pass interference: We've already mentioned pass interference, but it is a matter of such importance that it bears repeating. At all times, once the ball has been thrown or once the receiver is past you, you must play the ball and not the man. You're free to go after the ball for all you're worth, but you may not touch him in a manner that interferes with his right to make the catch. You already know when not to shove or push as you move downfield. Now, as the pass is coming down, you need to remember that if you first crash into the receiver and then try for the ball, the yellow flag will hit the turf immediately. There is also a good chance that interference will be called if the two of you go up for the ball and you then thump against him.

So remember the cardinal rule: Do everything you can to prevent the reception, but play the ball, not the man. You'll save yourself from having a pass called complete at the point of infraction, a "completion" that can prove disastrous on long throws deep into your territory.

Know your man: Every receiver will do all that he can to slip away from you and break into the clear. He'll present you with a kaleidoscope of fancy moves, cutting this way, sliding that way, faking still another way. Be prepared for any move, reacting quickly and accurately. One of the best ways to keep the receiver in check is to learn something about him beforehand. If possible, visit his home stadium and watch him in a game, studying him closely. Then, when you do at last face him, you'll have some idea of what he may have up his sleeve.

Tips

1. No matter your type of defense, never let the receiver move behind you.
2. Always backpedal when the play breaks, keeping your man in front of you and watching the quarterback.
3. On the bump-and-run, hit your man solidly to stop or slow him down; then run downfield alongside him. Do not look back for the pass until he does so.
4. Never let your man get behind you while you are deciding to try for the interception. Leap for the ball on interceptions, trying to catch it at its highest point as it drops to you.
5. Take care to avoid being called for pass interference.
6. If possible, study your receiver sometime prior to the game; learn his moves so that you'll be prepared for them.

12

BREAKING UP THE PLAY

The defensive stance: Many beginners think that a play is broken up only after the ball is snapped. Actually, the breaking-up process begins in the defensive huddle, when the strategy for handling the present game situation is determined. The process continues in the alignment, with every man knowing his place, his job, and the bit of ground he is to protect.

Even the stances taken by the men contribute to the breakup. The linemen drop into the three-point stance, ready to move forward or to either side quickly. The middle linebacker stands square to the line, hunched forward and able to charge or backpedal. The outside linebackers crouch with one foot slightly ahead of the other so that they can backpedal to their zones or their receivers all the more quickly. Farther back, the safeties face the line directly. The cornerbacks stand angling slightly to the outside. So stationed, they can move in swiftly on wide receivers coming down the sideline.

No matter your position, join every man in keeping your head up and your eyes open while in the alignment. Stay alert for any clue as to what the offense has in mind. Clues seen and acted upon do nothing but hasten the coming breakup.

Reading the keys: When the ball is snapped, continue looking for those all-important clues. Football men call them *keys.* They are movements that tip the hand of the offense.

For instance, suppose the offensive linemen charge ahead for more than a yard. Your football knowledge immediately tells you what's up. You know that they may not advance that far on a pass without being penalized as ineligible receivers. You're facing a run.

Or suppose the linemen drop back to throw a pass protection block. Prepare for the pass.

Or perhaps they pull out to the right or the left. Look for a run in the direction of their movement.

So that no key will go unseen, each defender is usually assigned to watch two specific opponents throughout the game. As each play breaks, he takes his clues from these men. Often one of the opponents moves in a way that suggests the direction of the play, while the second moves in a way that tips off the type of play.

Moving with the play: Though you must move quickly

once the ball is snapped, don't charge forward without thinking. Read your keys and react accordingly, but keep in mind the fact that the offense may be fooling you. For instance, the linemen may seem to be dropping back to protect the pass, but they may be only pulling you in for the draw. So stay alert. Think fast. Then readjust your play even faster.

If you're a linebacker or defensive back, be sure to develop the time-honored habit of dropping back a short step at the snap of the ball. This will give you the time to read the keys and take appropriate action.

Getting to the ball: When playing up on the line or just behind the line, you may always be certain of one thing: You're going to meet a block whenever you move toward the ball. Every successful defender employs individual techniques for getting around blocks, and you will need to develop a number of your own. Here, to get you started, are three long-used "antiblock" methods. Linemen find them especially helpful.

First, there is the *grab-and-shake* technique. At the snap of the ball, move forward immediately. Grab your offensive lineman by the shoulders, shake him, shove him in one direction, and then charge past him in the other direction. Speed and force are absolutely necessary for this maneuver. You must grab him before he has the chance to hit you. You must shake him hard and then shove him roughly to the side.

The *head slap* is an equally popular technique. Now, as the play breaks, slap the side of the man's helmet, knocking him to one side and leaving yourself an open path to the front. Quickness, strength, and accuracy are "musts" here. The slap must come fast, landing before the blocker makes contact. It must have the force to knock him aside. And it must be on target. If you miss, you'll throw yourself off balance and leave your midriff wide open for the block.

Finally, there is *looping*. Quickly step to the outside as the blocker charges. At the same time, bring your outside arm down and across your body, shoving the man away from you and to your rear. The entire action depends on quickness. The step to the side and the shove must come all in one movement. Incidentally, never shade yourself to one side of the man when setting yourself for the loop. He'll quickly figure out what you have in mind. Rather, take your stance nose-to-nose with him.

And take care in choosing the moment for looping. It should be used in passing situations only. It will leave you to the outside on runs to the inside.

Bringing the carrier down: Tackles are made from three directions: the front, the side, or the rear. Thanks to every carrier's elusiveness, the tackle from the front— the head-on shot—is something of a rarity. You'll have your chance to try it from time to time, though, especially if you're a lineman or linebacker. Most tackling in and beyond the secondary is done from the side or the rear.

When the chance comes for a head-on tackle, aim for the carrier's midsection. Run with your feet wide apart so that you are in good balance and able to shift quickly in either direction should he try to cut away. Then hurl yourself at him, striking him with the full surface of

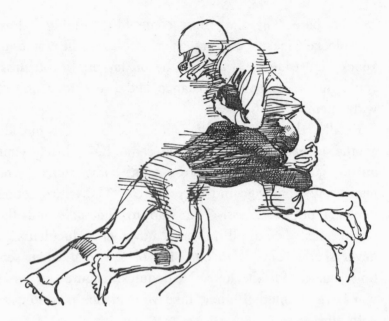

The head-on tackle

your shoulder and wrapping your arms about his legs. Pull his legs hard against you and drive him backward. Try to lift him off the ground.

With your shoulders aimed at the midsection, your arms should catch the man low on the upper legs. The closer you can come to his knees, the better. Unable to move his knees, he'll be deprived of the pumping action responsible for breaking many a tackle.

When approaching from the side or the back, take careful aim and, again, try to catch the man near the knees. On the tackle from the side, dive slightly ahead of the carrier so that your head and shoulder are in front of him. If you come in behind him, you'll give him the chance to spurt away from you.

Regardless of the direction in which you approach, there are certain fundamental rules that you must observe as a tackler. Learn them well, for they will help you bring your man down every time:

1. Keep your eyes open at all times. Closed eyes promise a missed tackle.

2. As in blocking, aim through the man. You'll then have the necessary follow-through for a truly strong tackle.

3. When pursuing the carrier, always try to force him toward the sideline or into the path of other tacklers.

4. Stop the carrier in any legal way possible. If you can't get a good shot at him, grab him in whatever way is left to you—around the neck, the shoulders, the chest. Push him out of bounds. Grab him around the arms if a lateral pass seems imminent. Stay away from illegal tackles, however. You may not grab the carrier's face mask, or tackle him once he has run out of bounds or after the whistle has blown.

5. Once you have your hands on the man, never let him go. Hang on, even if you end up just clinging to his ankle.

6. On every tackle, be alert for the fumble. As soon as you see the ball rolling free, go for it. Pick it up in any way possible. On many a play, your best bet is to dive atop the ball. Wrap it in your arms and hug it close to your body.

7. Have the desire to make the tackle at all costs. Go at your man aggressively. Half efforts invariably end in failure.

Tips

1. Take your proper stance in the alignment.
2. Read the keys correctly as the play breaks.
3. Develop the techniques for warding off blocks.
4. Learn and always use the fundamentals of tackling.

Mental and Physical Preparation

13

MENTAL ATTITUDES

Player qualities: To be of the greatest value to the team, a player must bring to the field something more than just the physical ability to play football. He must also bring certain mental attitudes—certain qualities—that will inspire him and his teammates to give the finest effort possible at all times.

Teamwork: The first of these qualities is a strong sense of teamwork. You must never forget, not even for an instant, that football is a team game. All eleven men on the unit—whether playing offense or defense—must work *together* on every play. All must co-operate, each doing his assigned job and helping the other. Otherwise, only a miracle will keep disaster from striking. So always be ready to co-operate to the fullest, no matter how you may feel at the moment. If you can't do this, then foot-ball is not the game for you.

Your sense of teamwork shows itself in many ways.

For instance, let's say that you're a running back, the fastest man on the squad. Yet you never try to "hot dog" it when you get your hands on the ball. You don't try to outrun your interference and then dazzle the crowd by single-handedly slipping, cutting, and faking your way downfield. Instead, you wisely pick up your blockers and let them clear a path for you. Only when they've done their job and fallen behind do you put on that final show of speed.

Or suppose the quarterback calls a play with which you disagree. You don't become angry and carry out your assignment halfheartedly. You get in there and do your job to the best of your ability.

Or you're a defensive lineman who thinks he should be a quarterback. You stifle your frustration, learn all you can about your position, and then play it for all you're worth.

If you see such signs of teamwork as these in yourself, treasure and develop them. Join them with the keen desire to play and win that all players must have. Your teammates will see the sense of teamwork that is in you and will always know that you are doing your utmost on every play. Every man around you will be inspired to work all the harder.

Confidence: You must go into every game with the confident feeling that your team will win. With this feel-ing strong in you, you will be able to play your best. But if you're sure that the team is going to lose, you'll actually work against yourself throughout the game, no matter how hard you seem to be playing. Without even knowing it, you'll perform poorly and lose just to prove that your suspicions were correct.

Confidence is made up of many different parts. There must be the feeling that your team is as good as the opponent, even better. There must be the feeling that your team can play harder and longer. There must be the feeling that your men can find the weaknesses in your opponent and take advantage of them. There must be the feeling that every one of your teammates knows his job. And the feeling that *you* know *your* job.

To many a player, that last point is the most important of all. To feel confident that you know your job, you must *actually know* the job, inside and out. So learn all that you can about football. Learn the rules of the game; know the penalties and how to avoid them. Learn how to play your position. Learn how to carry out every one of your assignments. Then practice and practice—and practice some more. You'll know when you're on your way to becoming an accomplished player. It will automatically do wonders for your spirit.

Just one word of caution: Avoid becoming overly confident. Always respect your opponent's abilities, and never think him easy to beat. Overconfidence quickly becomes arrogance. Arrogance leads to carelessness—and carelessness to defeat.

Enthusiasm: If the team is to win, every man must have what coaches call "hustle," the ability to play enthusiastically during every minute of the game. The enthusiasm of even one man is infectious. It spreads quickly to every member of the team, inspiring them all to a better effort.

Watch your enthusiasm as the game progresses. Football is a game of momentum. Sometimes the momentum is all with your team, and you seem to be able to do nothing wrong. But then, suddenly, everything changes. For the offense, perhaps there's a fumble, a broken play, or the failure to make a first down. For the defense, it may be a missed tackle or a successful pass out beyond the safety. Whatever the case, the momentum switches to the other side. Now you seem to be able to do nothing *right*.

When the momentum is with you, it's easy to play enthusiastically. But it's a different matter when the tide turns against you. Discouragement comes flooding in.

At such times, you must deliberately whip your enthusiasm to greater heights than usual. You must intensify your play, showing everyone that you know the game isn't yet lost and that you're doing all in your power to return the momentum to your side of the line. You must let no one, teammate or opponent, see a glimmer of the discouragement that's hidden within you. All this will encourage your teammates to work harder than ever. There is a good chance that the tide may then turn again in your favor.

And suppose that the tide doesn't turn. Suppose that, in the end, you lose. Again, remain enthusiastic. Figure out why you lost, but don't brood over the defeat. Learn from your mistakes and then quickly look forward to the next game. Prepare yourself for it, mentally and physically.

Aggressiveness: Football is a hard-fought game, with much body contact. Every man must play aggressively, blocking hard, tackling hard, running hard. If any man fails to do so, his opponent will knock him quickly aside and destroy the team effort. A win will never go into the record books.

Aggressive play is not to be confused with dirty play. Aggressive play is hard play, clean play, and heads-up play, with the player doing his best at all times and performing as the game demands he perform.

Many new players try to avoid aggressive play, thinking that they will then save themselves from being injured. They soon learn better. Aggressive play by a man who knows his position and how to handle it will actually help to avoid injuries. "Soft" play provides little protection against hard knocks. If you doubt the truth of this, ask any man who runs "softly" and then is hit full force by an opposing lineman.

Use your head: Today's football is not for the player who is mentally lazy. The number of plays that can be run and the number of defenses that can be taken all demand that you use your head at all times. Know your team signals. Listen for any signal change that switches the play or the defensive setup. Keep an eye open for weaknesses in your opponent and then take advantage of them. Stay with every play until the whistle blows. Be able to respond quickly to orders from the coach or the quarterback. When you're on the sidelines, follow the game closely so that you'll know the exact field situation when you're sent in. Never relax your thinking until you're back in the showers after the final gun.

Tips

1. Develop a strong sense of teamwork; carry out your assignment and co-operate with your teammates to make every play a success.
2. Gain confidence in yourself by developing your football skills to the utmost.
3. Avoid overconfidence, however. It quickly leads to arrogance.
4. Whether you're winning or losing, play enthusiastically.
5. If you lose, learn where you made your mistakes, but don't brood over the defeat; prepare yourself, physically and mentally, for the next game.
6. Play aggressively and cleanly; such play is necessary for a win and will help avoid injury.
7. Never stop thinking about the game until it's over.

14
PHYSICAL
CONDITIONING

Peak condition: Football is a rough game in which the body must move quickly and absorb many heavy blows. If you are to make the team and then play through the entire season, you must be in peak physical condition. Only then will you have the necessary strength for the body contact. Only then will you have the necessary stamina to last out the clock, remaining mentally alert all the while.

As a wise player, you should follow a year-round health regimen and not wait until the beginning of practice to get yourself into shape. Then you'll be able to launch into practice without unnecessarily straining your muscles and overtaxing yourself. You'll have the freedom to concentrate on sharpening your field skills and learning the plays.

So, in this chapter, let's look at a year-round health regimen.

Diet: Unless you have a weight problem, you need not follow a special diet. Rather, all you need to do every day of the year is make certain that you eat nutritious, well-balanced meals. Limit yourself to three solid meals a day, staying well away from fattening "in between" snacks of candy, cake, and such. Be sure that each meal includes a goodly share of vegetables. Chew your food thoroughly, preparing it for maximum use as fuel for the body.

Smoking and drinking have no place in the athlete's life. Each "drags down" the body and reduces stamina. Stay away from drugs, except those prescribed by a doctor for some ailment. Marijuana, LSD, and all similar drugs are to be avoided as if you were a running back and they a string of six-hundred-pound linebackers. And don't let anyone convince you that "pep pills" will get you "up" for a game. There's only one way to be "up" at the opening kickoff—and that's to be in top physical and mental condition.

Exercises: One of the best ways to stay in shape during the off-season is to participate in another sport. The choice of sport is entirely up to you. You may want to join in a team game such as baseball or basketball. Or an individual sport such as bowling, swimming, or hiking. The whole idea is to keep the body toned and ready for the coming season, avoiding the problem that troubles so many athletes—the softening of tissue and the loss of wind that occur when a period of idleness follows a season of activity. You must not only work hard to train the body in the first place, you then must work equally hard to keep it in shape.

Calisthenic-type exercises are excellent body conditioners. Push-ups, knee bends, alternate toe touches, and such will all serve to keep the muscles firm and supple. Certain exercises, however, are especially valuable for football players.

For instance, try running in place. The exercise works a number of muscles and builds stamina. Simply run in a standing position without moving forward. Breathe steadily and lift each foot at least six inches off the ground. First run to a count of twenty-five, counting once each time a foot strikes the ground. Then gradually increase the count to fifty or more.

Running backward is an excellent exercise for developing football agility and balance. From a standstill, run slowly backward for twenty to thirty steps, keeping in balance by riding your weight forward over your feet. Gradually increase the number of steps to fifty or more.

When you're at last on the practice field, you can continue to increase the number until you're traveling the whole length of the field. Always try to run in the straightest line possible.

Linebackers and defensive backs find the exercise especially helpful in developing their backpedal. Equally helpful is an exercise calling for a change of direction. Begin with a backward run, pretending that a receiver or a carrier is coming at you. Then pretend that he cuts to one side or another. Immediately cut with him. Run backward again and repeat the exercise several times, cutting in various directions.

This exercise is best done with a friend who serves as the offensive player. He runs at you and either turns or signals in the direction of the cut.

If you're a running back or a blocker, you can alter the exercise to your needs. Run forward, pretending that various tacklers are closing in from different directions. As a runner, cut or fake away from each. As a blocker, change direction to take the "man" out.

Again, a friend will be particularly helpful. Have him stand in the distance. Then, as you run toward him, have him point out the directions from which the imaginary tacklers are coming. If you're a running back, perform the exercise while carrying a ball so that you can practice shifting the ball to the side away from the tackler in a protective move against the fumble.

Additional ideas: When not practicing or exercising, always try to make life "a little hard" on yourself. Walk or jog to school or the store. Never ride in a car when you can get where you're going on foot or a bicycle. Stand and sit erect. Concentrate on holding your muscles firm. These everyday tasks will do much to assist diet and exercise in bringing you to and then keeping you in peak condition. They'll also add to the feeling that every player must have—the feeling of pride in himself and his appearance.

Incidentally, when first exercising, don't try to get back in shape all in one day. Too much exercise after a period of idleness strains the muscles and overtaxes you, canceling out much of the good that you're trying to do. For best results, start slowly with a few exercises, repeating each just a few times. Then, as time goes by, add new exercises to the list and gradually increase the number of times that each is repeated. You'll find yourself quickly and steadily toning the muscles and developing stamina.

Once you've begun your regimen, try your best to stick with it. Avoid any temptation to snack or forget your exercises for the day. If you do slip, make a fresh resolve to do better next time. Cap off each day with a full night's sleep.

Tips

1. Keep yourself in shape during the off-season by following a daily health regimen. Participation in another sport will help matters along.
2. Eat three well-balanced meals daily, avoiding fattening snacks in between.
3. Stay away from alcohol, tobacco, and drugs. Use only those drugs prescribed by a doctor for some ailment.
4. In the off-season, follow a regimen of exercises that will tone the muscles, build stamina, and develop agility and balance.
5. Never ride in a car when you can walk or pedal a bicycle. Train yourself to stand and sit erect, with the muscles held firm.
6. Stick with your regimen once you've started it, capping off each day with a full night's sleep.

15

KNOW YOUR FOOTBALL

Know yourself: No player can function on the field unless he knows the game of football, its rules, its strategies, and its penalties. He is completely lost unless he understands what is going on around him and why certain things are being done. So before ever going out for the team, you'll be wise to learn all that you can about the game. By reading books and watching games, fill your head with "football knowledge."

Football knowledge, however, is not limited to just the game, the rules, the strategies, and the penalties. It includes a knowledge of yourself—a knowledge of where you will best fit into the team and do your best playing.

There is no doubt that every beginner would like to

be a quarterback or a running back. These are the "star" positions, the ones that attract the most attention from the crowd. But don't try out for them just because they're so appealing. Rather, look closely at yourself and your abilities and then set your sights on the job most natural for you. Start by asking yourself some penetrating questions.

For instance, are you a fleet, powerful runner or a better blocker? Do you have good hands for pass receptions? Are you too small to play at a certain spot or too slow to play at another? Are you a good kicker? Do you get a particular thrill out of charging downfield under kickoffs? Are you defense- or offense-minded?

Honest answers to these and other questions will give you a good beginning idea of where you belong. You'll then help the coach immeasurably by trying out for the appropriate spot. You'll save him much time not only in deciding your position but also in determining whether you should play on offense, defense, or a special team. Once in your proper spot, the one most natural for you, you'll play at your happiest, even though a secret part of you may still want to be a quarterback.

Know the rules: The coaching staff will always have a set of rules handy. Study the rules closely and don't be afraid to ask questions about any that puzzle you. No one will think you stupid. The coaches want you to be sure of every rule.

It is a good idea to own your own rulebook so that you can consult it at any time. A rulebook can be purchased at practically any bookstore. If the store manager does not have one in stock, he'll be happy to order

it for you. An excellent rulebook with many helpful il-
lustrations in it is *Football Rules in Pictures,* edited by
Don Schiffer and Lud Duroska, and published by Gros-
set & Dunlap. At the time of this writing, its cost is
$1.95.

Know the officials: There are four, sometimes five,
officials on the field at all times. They keep the game
moving and spot infractions. You should know who they
are and the specific jobs for which each is responsible.
The officials are the *referee,* the *umpire,* the *linesman,*
the *back judge,* and the *field judge.* They are seen in the
following diagram in the positions they take at the start
of each play.

The referee is in overall charge of the game. His
duties include spotting the ball for the next play, signaling penalties to the grandstand, and pacing off penalties.
His decisions concerning play are final, except in cases
under the jurisdiction of another official.

The umpire is responsible for watching player conduct
and detecting illegal play. He also covers open play that
takes place after the initial charge of the linemen. Finally, he has primary jurisdiction over the equipment and
its condition.

The linesman marks the progress of the ball and
maintains a count of the down. Working under his direction, his assistants operate the yardage chains and the
down indicator. He keeps an eye on the neutral zone at
the line of scrimmage and watches for off-side infractions.

The back judge is used primarily in professional football, but he may also be found in some college and jun-

The official's positions

ior games. He is in charge of timing the game. He also watches for infractions in his area.

When the back judge is not present, the field judge takes over the timing of the game, starting and stopping the clock. He also serves as referee on plays that move downfield through the defensive secondary.

The decisions reached by the officials are final. Respect the decisions and do not argue with the officials. Arguments do nothing but delay the game and may upset some of your teammates so much that they will not play well until they've again calmed down. So concentrate on the game rather than on the feeling that you've been mistreated. And remember that incorrect calls are rare. Most officials do a fine job. They deserve your admiration and should be treated courteously at all times.

Know the official's signals: Officials use more than twenty-five gestures to signal penalties and the status of play to the players and the spectators. To avoid confusion and to avoid delaying the game by asking unnecessary questions, you should learn all these signals and be able to recognize them at a glance. Here they are now:

The ball is ready
for play

Start the clock

Time out. If this is an official time
out, rather than being charged
to one of the two teams, and it
occurs in a college or high school
game, the official then taps his
chest. In a professional game,
he taps his cap.

First down

Dead ball

Incomplete
forward pass

Safety

Touchdown. This signal is also used after a successful field goal or try for point-after-touchdown.

Off side. The penalty is five yards.

Illegal procedure. The signal indicates several different infractions, among them handing the ball forward and taking more than two steps after receiving a fair catch.

Illegal motion. The penalty is five yards.

Illegal shift. The penalty is five yards.

Illegal return. The signal indicates the return of a substitute previously disqualified, or before the completion of a down. The penalty is fifteen yards.

Delay of game. The penalty is usually five yards in high school and professional games, and fifteen yards in college games.

Personal foul. The signal indicates such infractions as piling on, tackling out of bounds, striking an opponent, and running into an opponent who is obviously out of the play. At the professional level, the referee indicates the precise foul after signaling the personal foul. The usual penalty is five yards.

Grabbing the face mask. This signal indicates one of the more often seen personal fouls. The penalty is usually five yards in amateur games and fifteen yards at the professional level.

Clipping. The penalty is fifteen yards.

Roughing the kicker. The signal indicates that an opponent has run into or otherwise interfered with the place kicker or the holder. The penalty is fifteen yards.

Unsportsmanlike conduct. The penalty is fifteen yards.

Illegal use of hands. The penalty is ten yards.

Intentional grounding of a pass. The penalty is five yards and a loss of down.

Pass or kick interference. The penalty is fifteen yards for offensive pass interference. When there is a defensive pass interference, the pass is ruled completed at the point of the foul. A fifteen-yard penalty is given for interference with the fair catch.

Illegal receiver downfield. The penalty is fifteen yards.

Illegal passing or handing the ball forward. The penalty is five yards and loss of down.

Illegal kicking, batting, or touching the ball. The penalties vary according to the infraction. Different penalties are used at the college and high school levels. Penalties are usually five or fifteen yards and can include loss of down or loss of the ball.

Know the penalties: As you can see in the preceding diagrams, most of the signals concern penalties. Penalties, involving much yardage lost or gained, play an important part in every game and can often mean the difference between a win and a loss. Consequently, many players try to take advantage of them by luring an opponent into an infraction. A prime example of this kind of play is the attempt to draw the opposition off side.

The strategy is considered good *if it works.* But it is also dangerous. Some coaches see it as far too dangerous, for, if you're caught trying to trick an opponent into a penalty, your side can be the one to end up with lost yards.

The best strategy for handling penalties is to know them and avoid them. Always remember that they can cost you the game. And never forget that many a penalty is there to deter the unsafe kind of play that easily results in injury.

Know the changing game: Football is a changing game. Plays with new wrinkles to them are constantly being tried. The rules are altered from time to time in an effort to make the game better. New and improved equipment continues to make an appearance.

In addition to knowing the game and your position, keep close tabs of all the changes in football. Keep abreast of all the modern developments. Think about this changing game and about what you yourself can do to make it even better. Who knows? You may be tomorrow's Vince Lombardi.

Tips

1. Know yourself; learn where you belong on the team and where you will be of best service.
2. Know the rules; don't be afraid to ask about any rule that you don't understand.
3. Know the officials and their signals; respect official decisions and treat the officials with courtesy and respect.
4. Keep track of the changes being made in football; think of what you can do to make it even a better game.

EDWARD F. DOLAN, JR., was born and educated in California, and has lived in that state for most of his life. After serving in the 101st Airborne Division during World War II, he was chairman of the Department of Speech and Drama at Monticello College, Alton, Illinois, for three years. While writing books for young people, he spent seven years as a free-lance writer in radio and television, and was a teacher for some years after that. His first book was published in 1958, and he has averaged a book a year since then, while continuing to do free-lance magazine writing and editorial work.

JOHN LANE, artist and illustrator, is chief editorial cartoonist of Newspaper Enterprise Association. His cartoons are distributed to NEA's more than 750 daily newspaper subscribers in North America. He joined NEA as a staff artist in 1956 and has been the firm's creative art director for the past six years. Since that time he has covered two presidential elections, including the national conventions, the races at Daytona, and several major trials, providing on-the-spot sketches of personalities and events.

796.33
DOL   Dolan, Edward F.

           Basic football
           strategy